W0017018

First and foremost, this book wouldn't be possible without God. For Your love, I am forever grateful. When the road gets lonely, You are my guiding light and firm foundation.

To my wife, Chelsea, I thank you for believing in me and encouraging me to follow this dream of mine. God has blessed me by putting you in my life and I hope you know that I love you... always have, always will.

To my babies, Sammy and Katcher, know that many of the morals and lessons that I have taught and plan to teach you are woven throughout this story. These words are meant for you to hold onto long after I am gone. From the moment you both came into my life I loved you and I will continue to do so through the rest of eternity. You are my sunshine. Let's change the world.

To my parents, thank you for encouraging me in my writing from a young age. It may have taken over thirty years, but here's the first installment of what will hopefully be a powerful and meaningful series. It is because of your love and support that this is happening.

To my grandmother, Margaret Katcher, I feel you with me every day. I love you Nana. It's through your spirit that we'll change the world.

To my niece, Taylor. Way back in 2001 when you were born, I was instantly drawn to the light you projected. From the first day I held you, I knew you would do great things. Let's change the world.

To my wonderful editors Sheila Shedd and Alex of Swift Creative, thank you so much for working with me as I put this story together. Your feedback was invaluable and I can't thank you enough for the lessons you taught me.

To Dave, Jaime, Max, and Bennett, you have all inspired me to pursue this dream. I love you all with my whole heart. Thank you for listening to my ridiculous rants, ideas, and for not losing hope in me as I worked through this process. You have all changed mine, so **together**, let's change the world...

Chapter One

The door to unit 21 was slightly ajar at the end of a dimly lit hallway in an apartment building that looked to be on the verge of being condemned. The numbers identifying the unit were barely hanging with the support of several stripped screws and to give credit where it is due...or not due, some masking tape. Nervously, the man approaching the door checks his cell phone for the time and hoping to see a message saying "Hey, man. I'm good. No need to come check on me." But Scott's phone had displayed no such message. Instead his eyes were met by the light of his phone and the clock display reading 3:12am.

Prior to placing his hand on the door knocker, Scott took another look down the hall down which he just journeyed. The dimly lit corridor was lined with six additional doors which were placed in a staggered pattern from each other. Scott envisioned the person who planned these floors as coming to this decision by placing his (or her) hand on their chin, looking up and down the hall, and saying "Nah, I wouldn't want to see my neighbors' face first thing in the morning, put the doors like this." Surely there were better lighting options than what was used in this hallway, Scott thought. Turning his head back to the mission at hand, Scott raised his right hand and gripped his fingers around the gold-plated door knocker that was affixed to the poorly painted door. As he did this, Scott noticed that the door was slightly ajar and now, an odor became prevalent and invaded his nostrils.

"Man, this is some bullshit." He said as he entered the department. As he walked in, the identity of the stench that met him at the entryway became identifiable now. That smell was unmistakable and belonged to... "Death. Ohhh God, it smells like death in here." Fighting the temptation to empty his stomach of the medium well steak, steamed carrots, and mashed potatoes he had for dinner several hours earlier, he closed the door behind him and flipped on the light switch to the left of the doorframe. Once the light spread across the room, Scott was relieved to see that there was no one lying dead on the floor or the disheveled sofa. But hey, this was just the living room of a three-bedroom apartment, there was still time, he thought.

As Scott surveyed the room, his eyes were drawn to the wall to the left of the television that hung on the wall. This wall was adorned with newspaper clippings and warm photos in nicely maintained frames that were hanging below a light focused solely on that area. It was as if this was the only area that his friend tended to in recent months. Not much dust or dander was to be found in a small radius surrounding the frames hung with such care. Scott walked toward the wall and was overcome with emotion as his eyes scanned over several of the photos.

Just over ten years ago, Scott was one of the thousands of "Specials" who formed a group which focused on protecting communities across the United States from threats "be they domestic, foreign, or not of this planet," as one of the clippings read. Scott was known as Flight. With a name like that, many people surmised that his name indicated the gift he was given was the ability to soar through the skies. Well, on the contrary, one of the powers that he was granted was invisibility. Scott liked to have fun with people and he did so when he chose his code name. The first photo Scott came across was taken at a neighborhood barbecue event with several other Specials who focused their downtime on the areas that were neglected by local officials.

In the photo, Scott was partially transparent and had a young child sitting on his shoulder that was still visible to others while he was smiling and looking to his left toward a broad young man in a spandex suit, which was the trademark of many of the Specials in that day. The man in which Scott was glancing at was pointing toward the camera with a smile that could have lit several city blocks. To the man's left was a woman with timeless beauty who was glaring lovingly at the man in the center while she was holding a little girl no older than 2 years.

Wiping a tear from his eyes, Scott continued to scan over the other photos and newspaper clippings. "Dante

Saves School Bus Full of Children," "Dante Flies to Arizona to Aid in Extinguishing Wildfire," and lastly "Mother and Young Child Among One Hundred and Twenty Killed in Explosion." Scott brought his right hand to his eyes and wiped away the rest of the tears. "Damn man, I didn't know that all this was in here. All you had to do was say something. Send a text, make a call, something," he said to himself as he shook his head. Scott grew up with the man known as Dante and had seen him grow into a national treasure prior to his sudden fall from grace after his wife and daughter were murdered in a what appeared to be a direct attack which took place at a heavily publicized event meant to benefit at-risk youth and families who were struggling to make ends meet.

Scott decided it was time to walk away from the photos before he spiraled down any further and began to move toward the sliding doors that gave way to the balcony. The sliding door was open enough to allow the wind to move the blinds covering the opening. Standing ever so still, he glanced around the living area of the apartment one last time.

The table that sat adjacent to a towering bookshelf was littered with pizza boxes, empty and crushed cans of beer, and unopened mail. The television on the wall was off, but there was a faint sound of music that was coming from down the hall, most likely from Dante's room.

Scott slid the door open just in time to see his friend leaning on the railing with one leg draped over the other side. "Dante, what the hell are you doing?!?" He yelled as he reached out to grab his friend before he plummeted 10 stories down. As Scott checked his surroundings, he saw that there were two empty bottles of Captain Morgan beneath the chair that his friend must have been sitting in.

"Scott, could you picture the headlines? Dante Attempts Suicide, but Forgets He is Invincible and Survives 10 Story Fall. What a joke. I'm invincible, but let what was most important to me die. They didn't deserve it, Scott. They didn't deserve to suffer that fate." Dante looked Scott directly in the eyes and with a tear sneaking from his left eye said "It should have been me." Scott blinked twice as if to try erasing the result of the attack from his memory. "You couldn't have changed anything. You weren't even there. Don't you dare put this on yourself!"

Pushing Scott back with a quick shove to the chest, Dante replied "That's the point, man! I wasn't around. I was never around. Yeah sure, for occasional photo ops, but never when it mattered. That's why they're not here anymore. It's my fault." Again, Dante pushed Scott away with just enough force to make Scott back into the sliding door. They both knew that if he wanted to, Dante could exert enough force to send his friend through the sliding door and through the other side of the building.

For a moment, Scott could see a fire in the eyes of his friend that he hadn't been seen a long time. Was it the alcohol or was his friend beginning to realize he was in a battle that is worth fighting? "Bro, I know it hurts. I responded as soon as I heard the blast. Some people hated the Specials so much that they wanted to chop us down by going at everything that made us human. I know it hurts, because I was the one who had to tell you what happened to your family. I know it hurts, because I had to carry out dozens of people who were killed in the blast. And most of all, I know it hurts because I loved them to!"

"But we don't get to run away and hide! We have to keep moving. We have a responsibility. You said it yourself. You've stewed in your own filth long enough. The city is in worse shape than it has ever been in and you're sitting up here drinking it away!" Scott grabbed Dante by the shoulders and looked him directly in the eyes. "It's time to do something about it. Those same people who took your family are poisoning the streets of the city you swore you'd protect and you're just wallowing in your own filth. Man up, Dante. We need you!"

As Scott released his grip, his gaze fell upon the skyline that just lit up as a result of another potential blast. "You can choose to do nothing and let another man feel the same pain you felt or you could grow a pair and bring the fight to the people who fired the first shot." As Scott delivered his message, Dante reached down and grabbed a bottle of

Captain Morgan which was not yet empty. Scott knew that

Dante had developed a drinking problem after the loss of his

family, but he did not realize the extent of the problem. Dante

pulled his arm back and launched the bottle deep into the

night sky. "Alright man, let's go" he said smiling with a similar

grin that was seen at the cookouts and block parties several

years before.

Chapter Two

Dante had been on his own most of his life. The young man's mother had passed away when he was just five, then on his thirteenth birthday, his once occasionally absent father decided to take on the role of full-time absentee father, beginning by making a trip to the grocery store and never coming back. Growing up in the very challenging neighborhood of Watts, California, Dante had few friends which he could truly confide in. Many of the kids his age were venturing into taking drugs themselves or selling and other gang activity, and Dante did not want to take part in anything that could bring harm to others. Somehow, he held out hope for his future, so he stayed with his small circle of friends, spending most of his time at the basketball court outside of the apartment complex he had come to know as home.

After Dante's father left, Scott Williamson's parents became Dante's temporary guardians. Scott and Dante had been classmates and very close friends since the third grade. Compared to the hectic and uncertain days that Dante was accustomed to, his time with the Williamson family was calm

and happy. Each day after school, Mrs. Williamson sat with

Dante and Scott and did homework before sending them off

to do chores as she made dinner for the family. The small two-

bedroom apartment was not much of a challenge for the boys

to tidy up as they waited for dinner to be served. One of

Dante's favorite memories during that brief period was the

wonderful aroma of homemade meatballs, pasta, and garlic

bread that Mrs. Williamson made every Monday night.

It was 2015; Dante and Scott were fifteen years old. On

one particular Monday afternoon, the old teal telephone

which was mounted on the living room wall rang, interrupting

a post homework cleanup session. "Dante, can you get the

phone?" Mrs. Williamson shouted from the kitchen. As he

removed the receiver from the wall, he could hear shouting.

Pressing the phone tightly against his right ear and covering

his left ear with his other hand, he heard Mr. Williamson

speaking frantically. "Scott? Dante? You have to get your

mother and get out of the house. You hear me boys? You have to get out of the…" Just then, the phone went silent and the lights began to flicker in the apartment.

"Was that Dad?" Mrs. Williamson asked as she stood in the doorway between the kitchen and dining room. Dante stood frozen, almost emotionless as he tried to muster up the strength to speak.

"Mr. Williamson…I mean Dad, said we have to get out of the house," he said, continuing to hold onto the phone.

"Oh…maybe he wants to meet for dinner. I've been making spaghetti and meatballs every Monday for what seems like forever…" she said with a smile, rolling her eyes as she approached Dante with her hand out for the phone. Scott entered the living room with his backpack slung over one shoulder. Just as Mrs. Williamson took the receiver, a loud bang from the front door startled everyone. As loud as the noise was, though, the light that burst through the opening was even worse. Three men, dressed in what appeared to be black military gear, charged into the apartment and approached Mrs. Williamson with weapons drawn.

"I need you to listen very carefully," said one of the men as he removed his helmet, revealing a face that looked like it was drawn for a comic book, a jaw square as a brick and a scar running from his forehead down to his right cheek. "I'm here for the boy, my boss has been looking for the one who is not yours. We truly do not want to cause harm, but he's going to need to come with us," the man said in a tone that was unnervingly relaxed. As this was going on, Dante grabbed Scott and dashed toward the closet in their bedroom. Once they arrived, Dante held his hand over Scott's mouth and leaned in close to his ear. "Scott, I'm sorry. I didn't know something like this would happen." As Dante was speaking, Scott was nodding his head up and down in agreement.

Shouting continued to come from the living room area as Scott and Dante remained hidden in the closet. "Listen, we have to get out of here. I'm going to make sure that you are safe, okay?" Dante said as he slowly removed his hand from Scott's mouth. With a terrified look on his face and tears in his eyes, Scott managed to nod in agreement to what Dante was suggesting. Dante flashed a gentle smile and nodded as he turned around and peered through the opening in the closet door. Suddenly there was a momentary silence in the apartment broken by footsteps marching in unison through the Williamson's home. One by one, doors were kicked open and the word "Clear!" was shouted as soldiers rummaged through one room and hurriedly moved on to the next. Near panic, Scott looked at Dante who calmly, Dante nodded again and readied himself as the footsteps closed in on their bedroom.

"Scott, darling," his mother called, her voice trembling, "these men just want to speak with Dante. That's all."

Scott reached to push the door open and Dante smacked his hand out of the way with a force that Scott had never felt before. With a red glare in his eyes, Dante shook his head and motioned toward the door, signaling toward the window that was on the opposite side of Scott's bed, five feet from the closet.

"Dante, I don't think you understand the scope of this situation or what is being asked of you," said another voice, deep and menacing, called from within the bedroom. "I am not going to continue asking you boy, I am now telling you. Come out now and no one else you love will get hurt." The men who accompanied him began rummaging through drawers outside of the closet. It was clear that they knew the boys were hidden there, but for some reason, they gave them the opportunity to emerge on their own.

"Let's go," Dante said as he grabbed ahold of his friend and fired through the closet door at the speed of a surface-to-air missile. The blast threw the closet door from its hinges and into one of the soldiers standing guard in the bedroom, startling the other soldiers, who'd clearly underestimated the strength of their target. Dante and Scott shot through the opening caused by the force of Dante, leaping from the closet, over the bed, and out the closed window at the opposite end of the room. Just as they passed the frame, Dante felt two sharp pains in his back, but nothing he couldn't ignore. He managed to look back to the hallway; one of the soldiers had pulled his weapon and fired at the boys. Assuming, wrongly, that he'd missed, he put a solitary shot in Scott's mother's head. Scott didn't see; Dante would be forever grateful for that. Years later, he would take solace in knowing that Scott had not seen his mother gunned down, minutes after his father had suffered the same fate.

As the pair of teenaged boys rocketed through the California sky, Dante's mind was strangely clear as he readied himself, preparing for whatever their next steps would be. Clearly, they had nowhere else to go, so what's next?

"Thanks, Dante. I mean it. If it weren't for you, I'd probably be toast," said Scott as he held on tightly to his friend.

"No problem, you'd do the same for me," Dante smiled.

"Yeah...except I can't fly. So, there's that."

"I didn't know I could," Dante yelled, glancing quickly down at the ground far below then back to the clouds.

Both boys laughed nervously, unaware of what fate awaited them.

Chapter Three

In the fall of 2016, a bumbling Dante was working as a waiter at a rundown restaurant located on a plot of weedy land which sat diagonally from a gas station that had long since been closed for business. Somehow, despite the practically barren wasteland surrounding this old-timey diner, it survived. In fact, it thrived in the face of seemingly insurmountable adversity.

During one particular dinner rush in which dozens of hungry patrons were staring intently at their menus, Dante was running between other waiters and bussers to serve his customers when his gaze fell upon a person he had not seen in the restaurant before. The way the fluorescent bulbs shown on her hair dazzled Dante in a way that he had never been dazzled before. The light seemed to bounce off her blonde hair, distracting him. One careless step back ultimately resulted in his crashing into a rushing server, and practically throwing a tray of Coca-Cola and water all over one of his regular's tables. The customers yelped and looked up at

Dante, shocked and angered, but Dante continued to stare at the girl, who was leaning on the counter ordering a strawberry milkshake and fries, while her two friends got burgers.

"*She's gorgeous*," he thought as he was desperately trying to clean the soda from the Jones' table and remember what the hell table 12 had ordered to drink. After he had cleaned up the best he could, Dante made his way through the busy dining area and to the kitchen. Frantically, he peered through the opening from the kitchen to the bar area and caught a glimpse of the girl who had caused him to drop the drinks which he'd so masterfully balanced on the tray he was carrying.

He briefly made eye contact and immediately felt the appropriate reaction would be to duck below the line of sight...even though, clearly, she had already seen him. Oh, how awkward and uncomfortable this moment was. Dante could not bring himself to go back out to the dining room. It was like this young man who could fly, bend steel, and was seemingly invincible was suddenly struck by a paralyzing fear of being seen by anyone.

Scott, who had been side by side with Dante since the incident with his parents, nudged the terrified waiter and nodded his head toward the dining area. Dante stared at Scott, unable to get a single word out of his mouth. Scott slammed his hands on the counter top and pointed at the stainless-steel swinging door which led to "Narnia," as Dante would later describe it.

"Seriously, dude! You're acting like a giant baby! Take the milkshake out there NOW!" Scott whispered loudly toward his best friend, using what Dante called his drama-queen face, overly expressive and contorted to near cartoon proportions.

Seeing this look from Scott always moved Dante to laughter – and action. He knew that it was time to man up and take that damned milkshake to the goddess. So, attempting to be as casual and confident as he could, he held the milkshake on the tray and made his way through the swinging door toward the counter seating area. As he took his strides toward her, Dante peered up from the tray holding her order to see where he was heading and at that same moment, the girl made eye contact with him again. "*Seriously*!?! Is she always looking up towards me or do I just not stand a chance?" he murmured.

"Yeah, bro..." Scott said from the kitchen window, "you just don't stand a chance." "You heard th..." Dante started to say as he looked over his left shoulder to see Scott nodding in agreement.

"Yeah, dude. I heard you. I'm pretty sure she might have heard you too," Scott smiled.

Nervously, Dante straightened his nametag and walked to the girl, who was holding her head in her hands and smiling. "No way she heard any of that." Dante said to himself as he approached confidently. Deepening his voice slightly, he said, "Here's your drink and fries, miss. Is there anything else I can get you? "And with a level of confidence he had never felt before, he set the food in front of the girl who had so successfully messed him up for the night.

Looking at him, smiling, she said, "Thanks, and yes, I did hear that. I heard alllllllll of that," as she took a sip of her freshly made milkshake and rolled her eyes. "And, by the way, my name's Martha...not 'miss.'" With that delivery, the girls who were flanking her laughed heartily and Dante slithered his way from the table which played host to the girl whom he would say "stole his heart at first milkshake."

As he made his way back through to the kitchen, Dante's eyes immediately made contact with Scott's. Scott had never been the type to hold back so, naturally, he instantly began badgering his friend. "So, you can lift cars, fly, and bullets literally bounce off of you, but you are petrified when a girl talks to you," Scott said smiling.

"No, I'm not petrified, just a little...um...yeah, nervous...that's it."

With that, Scott erupted with the type of belly laugh that resulted in his bending over and holding his stomach as tears began to well up in his eyes. "Well, did you at least get her name?" he asked as he was wiping the tears from his eyes.

"Yeah, bro. Her name's Martha."

Dante somehow seemed surer of himself than he had in the last ten minutes, Or *maybe*, Scott thought, in the last ten years.

"Why did you say that name!?!?!" shouted Steve, the cook who always chimed in with obscure movie references whenever the opportunity presented itself. This particular line was able to get a smile out of Dante and resulted in even more laughter from Scott. "Bro! Get it? *Batman Vs Superman*...MARTHA!" Scott managed to get out in between fits of laughter.

"Yeah man, I get it," Dante said as he peeked through the round window in the door as Martha and her friends got up from their seats and made their way across the black and white tiled floor and to the door with the golden handle. Dante began to walk toward where the girls had been sitting and started to clean up the glasses and wipe down the bar counter. As he was meticulously cleaning the bar surface, he felt a hand on his left shoulder.

"Hey. I think you forgot something," said the sweet voice. Startled, Dante turned around and saw Martha. The lights hanging from the ceiling of the diner shined on her in a way that illuminated her and made it appear, to Dante, anyway, as if she was the only person in the building.

"Uh, yeah? What did I forget?" he asked nervously, switching halfway through to that ridiculous, deep voice that he'd never used before.

"Well, Slugger," she replied, "you forgot to ask when I was free to get a bite to eat." Her smile that reached deep into his heart and took hold like nothing else had been able to.

Scott was walking by to deliver a tray of food to another table and as he passed, he leaned in and quietly whispered, "Focus, dude. Focus."

This moment of encouragement brought Martha to smile some more and Dante finally summoned the courage to string enough words together to form a sentence, or something that slightly resembled a sentence. "Free for food?" he blurted out as if he was unable to process what had just happened.

Scott, who was easily twelve feet away at this point, but had still heard this masterpiece of words, burst into laughter again.

"Look, here's my phone number. Give me a call when you get some time." Martha wrote her phone number on a napkin sitting on the countertop. Taking Dante's hand for a brief moment, she placed the napkin in it and closed it gently, letting her hand linger for just a moment longer. "Well, I guess I'll be hearing from you soon, Slugger." She turned and made her way toward the door to reunite with her friends, who were giggling madly as they exited the diner.

In that brief moment that she'd held his hand, Dante experienced a feeling that he had never felt before. A mixture of vulnerability, bewilderment, and anticipation. This girl, who moments earlier had made him feel so anxious and nervous, had suddenly made him feel so at peace. Grinning widely,

Dante slid the napkin into the pocket of his black jeans and continued to clean the counter.

Almost as if he was on a cloud, he floated through the swinging door which and placed the tray gently into the three-compartment sink. Steve, who had been minding his own business, stared at Dante who was literally floating inches off the floor.

"What the f---?!?!" he said as he experienced firsthand, a small glimpse at the power that Dante held within. What seemed to be a shy, reserved young man, was a being who was powerful beyond comprehension. With his jaw hanging wide open, Steve dropped the utensils he was holding and Scott burst through the door as Dante continued hovering slightly above the floor.

"YOOOO! You got the digits!" Scott yelled at him, holding his hand up for a high-five.

Maybe it was that Dante was floating in the air; maybe it was the nonchalant way in which Scott was interacting with the person who was *floating in the air*, or maybe it was the two joints he'd smoked before his shift. Who's really in a position to judge? Steve took one last look at his hovering co-worker and collapsed to the kitchen floor and landing with a thud that reverberated throughout Narnia.

Chapter Four

For Dante, life had meant facing an unending string of challenges. His mother dying so young, his father leaving, then the terrifying upheaval at the Williamson's had put him face to face with some of the most difficult scenarios imaginable. Dante had had more than his fair share of adversity. But instead of crumbling under the immense pressure and trauma, the young man persevered and continued pushing forward.

Days after his momentous interaction with Martha at the diner, Dante came in contact with the first of many adversaries. This "Special," as super-powered people were known, discovered the existence of him and was drawn to him by the cook who had passed out at the sight of Dante floating in the kitchen. Once Steve woke up from his spill, Dante and Scott tried to convince him that he did not see Dante floating, but imagined the whole thing, probably as a result of the weed he'd smoked before his shift started. Steve shrugged it off and played coy with the pair, seeming to agree. But when he left the diner and made his way home, he would spend some time in several online chat rooms.

Upon arriving at his parent's home, Steve dropped his backpack at the door and started making his way up to his room. "Young man!" yelled his father from across the house. "You better kick those shoes off and hang that backpack up before you go stomping up those stairs!" Steve's dad had the uncanny ability to sense when one of his children were breaking a house rule. Shoes past the entry way was one line that was not to be crossed. Almost embarrassed, Steve took off his Jordan's and placed them neatly along the wall. He then picked up his black Nike backpack and hung it gently on the oak coat rack. Without missing a beat, Steve's father chimed in with a pleasant, "Thanks, son."

Smiling, Steve grabbed the white painted railing and began to ascend the stairs quickly. Grasping the bronze door knob, he twisted it and in one seamless motion, he spun, flipped on the light switch, performed another, slightly clumsier spin, and dropped into his gaming chair. Once he recovered from his barrage of spins, he kicked his way to the desk, which was the home of his laptop, and began tapping away at the keys. Convinced that he had not imagined Dante floating in the diner kitchen, he began to search for phenomenon of that sort. To his surprise, the screen lit up with hundreds of results featuring descriptions of similar events taking place all over the world. The results spanned a wide variety of topics, from people who ran faster than the eye could see, to individuals somehow stopping speeding buses with one hand and moving a child out of harm's way with the other, always coming away unscathed while saving the passengers and bystanders.

Steve's eyes lit up with the thought of the notoriety he would pick up if he shared the story of how he saw his coworker floating in the dingy kitchen of the run-down diner in which he worked. So, without much hesitation, he began to type his firsthand account. Now, this account may have included several exaggerations, but it was easy for him to come up with the details, so why not add a little excitement?

Soon, his imagination ran wild, and, as a result, he crafted some additional "eye-witness accounts" that he borrowed from his many hours spent reading comic books and watching movies. Some of the stories were pretty far-fetched; there was the Special who had stopped a speeding car with one hand, and another about an individual who ran past him at a speed that would make most cheetahs jealous. Steve pecked away at the keyboard, his face illuminated by the soft green lights emanating from beneath the keys.

His finger lightly tapped the mouse as it was hovering over the "submit" icon. In his mind, this was the only course of action to take. Steve's thoughts began to wander and he imagined being invited onto talk shows to discuss the incredible events he saw unfold with his own eyes.

The daydream scenario continued and expanded to the national news reaching out to him to speak about what he thought should be done to control the Specials and their powers. Gazing off into the distance, Steve imagined himself inside a studio facing several cameras and heavily powdered television personalities who were just dying to talk to this new media darling.

"Tonight, we're joined by Steve, the young man who alerted the masses to an influx of individuals who possess powers that eclipse those of a typical human being. Right, Steve? For example, one of your closest friends is one of these "Specials" that you thrust into the spotlight. Dante...that's his name, right? The one who can hover in thin air and serves milkshakes flying through the diner you both work at." The host nodded her head as she stared at Steve, who was sitting a few feet away from her and dabbing sweat from his forehead.

"So, tell us, Steve. What drove you to push a person whom you claim as your friend to the forefront of an inevitable assault from a society which fails miserably at accepting those who are different, whether in appearance or ability?"

The camera operator shifted his focus from the host to Steve's face and zoomed in to a point which was uncomfortably close. Steve glanced at the host with a quizzical look on his face and then looked out toward the studio audience who were looking directly at him with doubting, disapproving glares. Nervously, Steve reached into the box of tissues which sat on the glass table between him and the host. His shaking hand grasped a tissue and he wiped it across his forehead and tried to speak, but he was unable to produce an answer.

Pouncing quickly on the opportunity that presented itself, the host continued with her line of questioning. "I see what's going on here. You wanted fame and notoriety for what you felt was 'your' discovery, eh?" With that delivery, the host offered a half-smile and shook her head as she looked toward Steve, who was sinking down into his seat.

"Is the death of thousands the fame you were looking for? I mean, really, Steve. Thousands. You have created a snowball effect which will impact generations, not just the people who are in the range of the immediate 'celebrity' that you'll gain from your reveal. You have created a ripple effect that will only be corrected by devastation and destruction.

You. Did. This." The host then placed her note cards on the

table and stood up from her chair.

With a look of confusion and worry on his face, Steve

grasped both arms of the chair and could not take his eyes off

of the host, who was getting progressively angrier and more

confrontational. As the general disapproval grew from the

audience, the host clinched her hands into fists and, almost

instantaneously, her hands began to glow and emit a white

fire from them.

Looking into Steve's face, the host screamed out "Do

you hear me, Steve? You did this! Do you hear me?!?!?" As

the fire and glow spread from her hands to her eyes, Steve

finally mustered the strength to lift himself from the chair

which had just played his personal prison for the last ten

minutes of questioning. Members of the audience began to

get up from their seats at the sight of the host who was

apparently one of the "Specials" that Steve had exposed.

Instinctively, the audience members stampeded towards the

exits at the top of the stairs, and, in the blink of an eye, the host extended her hands and sent a blast of light toward both exit doors, causing an explosion that sent multiple members of the fleeing audience into the air and back toward the stage.

"This is bigger than you, Steve. But you fail to see that because you let your ego get in the way. Those people died because of you. And they will not be the last. Their blood is on your hands. Feel famous yet?" The host then put her hand out toward Steve's face which was now completely saturated with sweat. "Do you hear me, Steve? Do you?!?"

"Steve, are you okay, son? Can you hear me?!?" Steve's father was shaking his shoulders as he shouted to get his son's attention.

Wearily, Steve opened his eyes and stared quizzically at his dad. Looking around, he smiled, realizing he'd only fallen asleep at his desk. Steve nodded his head as a response to the question being posed to him.

Blinking rapidly and wiping the sweat from his brow, Steve looked down at the words on the screen of his laptop.

Without much of a pause, he depressed the "'discard"' icon on the screen, closed the laptop, and looked up at his dad. "Yeah, dad. I hear you."

Chapter Five

August 2017. The Clatsop State Forest, located in the Northern Oregon Coast Range, is a sprawling landscape which spreads across one-hundred thirty-six thousand acres. Deep inside the forest stands a heavily guarded government compound that is surrounded by chain-link fence topped with barbed wire, search towers with large spotlights, and armed guards scanning the perimeter of the fence.

On the eighteenth floor of the facility, Charles Wingard, Director of Special Operations peered out the window and squinted briefly before turning around quickly to grab the binoculars from his desk. Pressing the binoculars against his eyes, he scanned the darkness of the forest beyond the fencing and spotlights.

"Son of a bitch," he mumbled quietly to himself. He continued to look out into the distance that lay beyond the safety of the facility that he had made his home away from home. Nervously and with shaking hands, he stepped away from the window, reached down to the top right drawer of his desk, pulled it open and gently replaced the binoculars with the standard issue firearm supplied to him by the government. As he made attempts to regain his composure by breathing in and out deeply, he slid the weapon into his belt along his waistline.

The silence in his office could only be matched by the silence in the forest that lay on the other side of his window. Wingard made his way from his desk to the bookshelf that stood waist high on the other side of the room. He knelt down and slid several books on the bottom shelf to the side and revealed a half empty bottle of whiskey and a glass that had his initials etched in it. Forgoing the glass, he stood back up, spun the cap off and took a swig, right as the unnerving silence was abruptly interrupted by the ringing of his cell phone.

"Wingard, here," he said as he placed the bottle on his desk and slid his chair out to take a seat.

"Subject seventy-two is exhibiting combative characteristics and we require your presence in the research wing."

Wingard sighed and confirmed he would be on his way. He put his phone back on into his pocket and spun his chair around to look out the window again. Several trees began to bend in a wavelike pattern, as if someone or something was running by them and causing the trees to move. "Get it together Wingard," he said as he slapped his hands on his cheeks and took one last swig of the whiskey before returning it to its hiding place on the bookshelf. As he moved toward the office door, he grabbed his suit jacket from the coat hanger to the left of the door and put it on. He switched the light off and exited his office, making his way to the elevator down the hallway.

Passing several individuals wearing lab coats, Wingard boarded the elevator and made the descent to the basement level, which housed the Research Wing of the facility. This particular area played host to a number of labs which were dedicated to various stages of scientific research and some were classified, he thought perhaps even questionable, experiments. As he exited the elevator, Wingard turned right and strode down a dimly lit hallway which compared to what was happening through some of the doors on either side, was quiet...peaceful, even.

Wingard reached into his left pants pocket and retrieved his identification card which granted him access to the Research Wing. Almost as soon as he passed through the doorway, he was greeted by a research specialist who grabbed ahold of his arms.

"Thank god!" he said. "I have never seen a reaction like this before. Please, come," the scientist said, already making his way toward an observation room.

Grabbing the file that was hanging on the outside of the room, Wingard hurried in after him and closed the door behind them. "What do we have here?" he asked as he flipped through the chart.

"Subject Seventy-Two began to exhibit hostile traits shortly after twenty-three hundred. With this type of treatment, the reaction shown is typically short lived. But there was something different with this one." As he was speaking, the man was operating a computer which displayed a security camera feed. Once the footage stopped rewinding at 11:14pm, the man let the video play at normal speed. Initially, not much happened, but then the subject's movements quickly changed.

The man known as Subject Seventy-Two was being held captive and had been for quite a few years after being plucked from what seemed to be a relatively normal life. That "normal life" was disrupted when certain DNA markers indicated that he bore genes that differed significantly from the typical human being. In a top-secret operation, he was just one of dozens who had been identified, gathered and caged inside this compound, held by the covert organization known as the Department of Human Deviations for "additional research." As Wingard and the scientist continued to look at the screen, Subject Seventy-Two looked directly at the camera and seemed to be speaking, though what was being said was said was inaudible to the camera.

"Close in on his face. Take the camera as close as it can go without distorting the image," Wingard commanded as he leaned in closer over the chair in front of him. The Specialist did as he was asked and was able to get the image blown up to a size that allowed both men to see Seventy-Two's scarred face clearly. "What the hell did he just say?" Wingard mumbled as he motioned to the Specialist to rewind the footage. As they watched the footage again, Wingard stood up and stiffened in his stance. "Dammit...I'm pretty sure he said 'lights out.' That can't possibly be good. Quick, get to the panel and initiate security protocol ten..." Just as Wingard was issuing his new set of commands, the main power of the facility went out and was quickly picked up by the emergency power generator.

Nervously, the research specialist looked at Wingard for guidance and just as soon as their eyes moved from one another's, there was a sound of an explosion from somewhere in the facility. Wingard pulled his weapon from his waistband and silently motioned for the Specialist to get to the floor and move beneath the desk. Both men were frozen in place, intently focused on the security monitor. In an instant, the stillness of the room was broken by a blast that emanated from the wall behind the monitor. The force was so strong that it sent Wingard airborne, launching him into the wall across the room. Dazed and injured, but unable to determine just where the injury was, Wingard fixed his eyes on the massive opening in the cell wall where the security monitor had just been.

Slowly, methodically, and intently, a figure began to materialize through the dust and haze still hanging in the air. The figure made its way through the opening and was soon flanked by two additional entities. The lights in the observation room were flickering at this point, and Wingard squinted his eyes in an attempt to make out who or what was standing in front of him. Cutting through the silence was a booming voice, deep enough that it echoed between the two rooms. "What's wrong, Charles? Didn't you want to see us up close and personal? Oh, that's right...you would prefer to have us in restraints, in another room... tucked safely away from you," the man said as he looked at the individuals beside him and raised his arms to shoulder level.

"Seventy-Two, right? That's what you all called me. 'Subject Seventy-Two. You took me from my family, stripped me of my name... most of my memories, and gave me a code-number to dehumanize me...to reduce us to lab rats. That's where you went wrong, Charles. We are human; well, maybe not in the typical sense of the word. But we represent what is best about humanity, what is better, and you just could not let us live our lives. You did this, Charles. Directly or indirectly, you are responsible for what happens tonight when we leave this hell hole." Seventy-Two began to walk toward Wingard, and in his strides, he gestured beneath the desk to the two men who were with him. At that moment, they quickly closed in on the research specialist and lifted him from his hiding spot.

As Seventy-Two stepped toward Wingard, he saw a flash of light and a scream was cut short as the research specialist was evaporated in an instant. Wingard drew his gun but was just a second too late as Seventy-Two kicked it from his hand, just out of his reach. Seventy-Two tilted his head slightly to the left as he took notice of Wingard's injured hand. "A wedding band?" Seventy-Two asked as he reached down, grasped Wingard's wrist, and lifted him violently from the ground. "Do you have children, Charles? I had a child; I can recall that much. But I'm not telling you anything you don't already know, right? You know all about my son AND my beautiful wife, don't you?"

Wingard nodded his head, but refused to make eye contact with Seventy-Two. Nodding his head in controlled anger, Seventy-Two pulled Wingard closer to his face and ran a finger along the scars that lined his face. "I missed her while you and your 'Research Specialists' poked and prodded me and the others. I would have given anything to see my family again. But I can't see ever them again...not like this. Not after what you've done to me. You made me a monster, Charles. You'll die, but I have to live up to the expectations that were set for me. Judging by the look on your face, you fail to realize just what you have accomplished. Soon everyone will learn of the mistakes that were made here."

Seventy-Two shifted his gaze again to Wingard's wedding band. "Will they miss you?" he asked, almost to himself as he released his grasp on Wingard's wrist, thrust his right hand forward, and emitted an energy blast that created a hole in the center of Wingard's chest and an opening in the exterior wall and right through the security fencing. "I guess you'll never find out."

Seventy-Two and the others flew through the hole and into the night sky above the forest beyond the compound, escaping the prison that held them for so long, embarking now on a new and frightening journey before them.

After what seemed like a prolonged delay, guards finally arrived at the door to the observation room with weapons drawn; all they could do was survey the damage. One solider bent to check Dr. Wingard's failing pulse.

"Get them back," he wheezed. "We must get them back."

Chapter Six

As time passed and their relationship grew stronger and Dante and Martha enjoyed their fateful interaction in the diner, Dante had made it a priority to keep in contact with her at least once a week. But between his coursework at the local community college and work at the diner, he rarely had a free moment to be with her in person. As the months rolled by and winter transitioned into spring, Dante found himself more enamored with Martha than when they'd first met and she'd passed him her number on a damp napkin.

It was a beautiful spring day in March of 2017, and Dante had asked Martha to go out on just their second date. They hadn't been on an official night out since the previous November when the pair attended an ice-skating party at the indoor rink, tucked away in the center of the suburbs. Internally, Dante wrestled with the reasons why he did not ask Martha to go out more frequently early into their relationship. He knew the powers that he had could put her and others right in harm's way, so he told himself, and Scott, that she would be better off without him in her life. But whenever his phone would alert him to a new text or incoming phone call from her and her picture filled the screen, he would become overtaken by a euphoria that he had not experienced much to this point in his life. So, finally, he looked past his own self-driven fear and anxiety and built up the strength to plan their second date.

Dante toiled over details in order to make his evening with Martha perfect. Leading up to the big night, he monitored the weather reports, bought a new outfit to wear, and made a reservation at the restaurant that Martha told him was her favorite in town, but that she had not been to since she was a little girl. Dante got into his older, navy blue Chevy Chevette, pulled the door shut, and grasped the steering wheel tightly. He turned his head slightly to the right and looked at the empty passenger seat and a vison of a laughing, glowing Martha burst into his mind. Smiling, he shook his head to bring himself back to reality, started the car, and began his drive to Martha's home.

The news was on the radio: "The apparent covert operation that took place last fall and resulted in the death of Director of Special Operations Charles Wingard and several others in an Oregon military compound is still under intense scrutiny as protesters gathered outside of the White House this afternoon looking for answers. Many of those who came to peacefully protest asked the same questions: 'What really happened?'

With that final line, Dante turned the radio off and pulled up the driveway beside Martha's home. Putting his vehicle in park, he glanced up toward the front door where Martha was seated on a swing at the far end of the porch. Dante found himself getting lost in the moment; Martha was slowly gliding back and forth, the wind blew gently, tossing her slightly and the afternoon sun illuminated her face in a way that made Dante believe that this...*this* is what Heaven must be like, and that angels do, in fact, exist.

After a moment, Martha saw Dante sitting in his Jeep in the driveway and she was hit by the undeniable urge to smile. She reached down to grab her purse, yelled in through the front screen door to let her parents know that she was leaving and made her way down the stairs to Dante. His gaze did not break from her direction and as she approached his door. He put his window down and she leaned on the opening. "Hey there, Slugger," she said, and started for the passenger side of the car. Doing his best to resist the urge to burst into full "super-duper speed" as Scott called it, Dante jumped out of the car, and rushed to the passenger side, and opened the door for her in a very normal, ordinary person manner. Martha nodded her head and grabbed Dante's outstretched hand, stepped up, and sat in the passenger seat.

After dinner, Dante and Martha decided that they would go for a walk downtown. The sun was beginning to set and the roads that ran below the towering buildings adorned with ancient gargoyle sculptures were empty because of a re-election event for the mayor which was occurring several blocks away. Many in the city wanted more answers than what the feds were willing to give in regards to the events in Oregon several months earlier.

"So, do you believe any of the things that they're saying about the attack in Oregon?" Martha asked as they were walking.

"Well, there's a lot being said by a lot of different people. It's hard to cut through the static to see what is real," Dante replied.

The couple reached a park in town and took a seat at one of the benches that was facing the city. The buildings were glowing from the setting sun behind them. Martha moved closer to Dante and leaned into his side. As Dante looked toward the buildings, he interlocked his fingers with Martha's. The trees were gently swaying in the wind but that stopped suddenly and the birds, chirping just moments before fell eerily silent.

A few minutes later, four police cruisers filled the silence by speeding by with their sirens blaring and lights flashing. Martha tightened her grip on Dante's hand and an explosion lit up the sky ten miles away. In an instant, Dante stood up from the bench and grabbed Martha's shoulders as he scanned the scene behind her in the park. Dante noticed an officer walking near the restrooms on his way through and urged Martha to make her way to him.

"What do you mean?!? What are you going to do?" Martha asked, raising her voice. Brushing her hair from her face, Dante smiled. "I'll be right back," he said as he handed her the keys to his car. Stepping up on her toes, Martha gently kissed him on the cheek and turned to run toward the officer.

Dante began to sprint toward the site of the explosion as others were running the opposite direction. This gave him a comforting feeling because he knew that Martha was going to be safe with the officer, away from the blast point. Sighting a break in the panic, Dante jumped from the street and took flight over the crowd, who because they were so intent on running from what just happened, did not observe him above them. Closing in on the site, Dante could see that the explosion came from just outside of the re-election rally.

Bodies were scattered all over the street and significant damage had been done to vehicles and buildings across from the courthouse steps where the podium was set up for the mayor to make his pitch to the crowd. Dante descended to street level and tucked himself beside a vehicle which was already on fire, trying to see who was standing on the other side of the flames and smoke.

"You know damn well why we're here," a deep voice shouted from through the fire. "You and people like you brought us to this point. Oregon was just the beginning. We will not be silenced, and we will not be used," the deep voice shouted from within the flames.

Hunched down low, Dante moved ahead and stepped through the dancing flames and black smoke. "Stop right there!" he screamed with a slight tremble in his voice. Without hesitation, the man who was shouting turned around and sent an energy blast directly in Dante's direction. The blast hit his chest, ripped his shirt, then dissipated around him. Dante remained standing.

A masked Seventy-Two looked quizzically at Dante and raised himself from the ground while pointing for the two others who were with him to stay with the mayor. "Boy, I don't know if you truly grasp what you have put yourself in the middle of. This does not concern you," Seventy-Two declared as he raised both of his arms at his side which resulted in the pavement in front of him to erupt in waves towards Dante.

Instinctively, Dante launched himself into the air. He made contact with Seventy-Two and the two soared through the air and into the side of a building away from the blast point. Dante took a piece of his ripped shirt and quickly wrapped it around his face in a last second attempt to conceal his identity.

Once his face was obscured from sight, he grabbed a piece of the concrete which was crumbling as a result of their impact into the building and slammed it into the side of Seventy-Two's head.

"Not bad," Seventy-Two said as he straightened his rigid, black mask. "I think that this is just the beginning of our relationship, young man. I'll be seeing you very soon." With a quickly placed kick to Dante's chest, Seventy-Two ascended into the sky and called for the beings which were with him and they made their exit from the area.

Reacting to his adrenaline, Dante wanted to go after the trio, but realized that there was more to be done here. He changed his course and flew toward the mayor as sirens and the sound of helicopter propellers filled the air. Reaching down with his right hand, he grabbed the mayor by his arm and took him into the air, setting him safely back down two blocks away.

Unable to get words out, the mayor mouthed a "Thank you" to Dante as a car horn began to blare from behind them. Dante turned his attention from the mayor and saw the vehicle, which was now flashing its high beams, coming toward him. The mayor began to run away toward the security detail and police who were setting up around the corner.

Much to Dante's surprise, Martha leaned from the driver's side window and looked directly at him. "Get in! I think we have some things to talk about!" she yelled as she got back into her seat, leaned over, and opened the passenger side door, signaling for Dante to hurry.

Dante got in, removed the tattered shirt from his face, grinned coyly and said "Yeah, I guess you're right."

Chapter Seven

As they drove onto Martha's street, the two remained in an uncomfortable silence that built into a tension that could probably be felt from outside of Chevette. Pulling into the driveway of her parent's house, Martha placed the car in park and turned her head to Dante, who, with the exception of his ripped and torn shirt, seemed unscathed by the altercation he had just found himself at the center of. As Martha tried to coherently form a statement that might begin to answer the many questions she had, the porchlight turned on and her parents burst from the front door.

"Guys, we're okay! I'll be up in one minute," Martha yelled to her visibly shaken parents, who stopped at the edge of the porch, just before reaching the top step. Her father awkwardly raised his hands above his head and took several steps back toward the door, spun, grabbed the screen door handle, and ushered his wife back into their home.

"So, what else can you do?" she asked as she gently settled her chin into her hands and leaned forward on the center console. Dante was struck with the urge to lie about his abilities, but there was something about Martha that made him unable to be anything but completely and absolutely truthful with her.

Taking a deep breath and settling into the passenger seat, he rattled off his list of abilities that went from flight and "super-duper" speed to what seemed like invulnerability. "How long have you had these…powers?" Martha asked, stunned by what she was being told.

"For as long as I can remember. Some of the abilities rose to the surface later than others. But, even when I was little, I can remember having the unenviable task of trying to hide what I was from everyone around me," he replied to her as he continued to make eye contact, finding himself lost in her gaze.

As they sat there, they both noticed the not-so-subtle hint of the porch light being turned off then on again in a signal for Martha to come inside. "I'll walk you to the door." Dante said as he reached for the handle.

"Um...your shirt," Martha laughed as she reached out to stop him from exiting the vehicle. Almost as if he'd forgotten that his shirt was in tatters, Dante looked down at himself and nodded in acknowledgement. "It was a nice gesture, though," she smiled. "Very gentlemanly. Maybe on our next date, we can do something not so dangerous. You know, like...see a movie or play some mini-golf." She kissed him quickly on the cheek and opened the door.

"Our next date? You're not scared?" Dante asked, genuinely surprised. Closing the driver side door gently and leaning on the window opening, Martha replied to him with a reassuring response. "I'd be lying if I said that tonight wasn't terrifying, but I like you Dante, I really like you. I would love to have a 'next date' with you." She winked at him just before the front door opened again and a loud "Ahem" emanated from the inside the house. "See you later, Slugger," she said and, walking up the steps to the porch, she disappeared into the house.

Now fully aware of the shirtless situation he found himself in, Dante shifted himself from the passenger seat to the driver seat and backed his old, faithful Chevette out of the driveway. Driving through the darkness, his mind began to wander back to the terrible events of earlier in the evening. So many people were hurt or killed in what seemed to be a senseless act of terror. However, this act had been committed by others with abilities similar to his. This meant that he was not the only person with special abilities. And now there was a sense of dread that came along with that realization. Sure, he fell on the "good-guy" side of the spectrum, but the public wouldn't know that. He could easily be lumped in with those who were clearly on the opposite side of things.

Pulling up to a stop sign several blocks from his home, Dante's mind continued to churn out scenarios and possibilities about what could come next. Wiping the sweat from his brow, he gently placed his foot on the gas, yet was unable to move the vehicle forward. A thud came from the back of the car which made Dante shift his focus to the rearview mirror. As his gaze met the mirror, it made contact with a glowing red pair of eyes at the back of the vehicle. As quickly as they appeared, the eyes were gone, but the inability to move his car remained. In a flash, the driver side door opened and Dante was snatched from the vehicle and slammed to the ground beside it.

With the wind knocked out of him, Dante looked up and was surprised to see Seventy-Two glaring down at him. "Young man, you have no idea what you did tonight. You made the spotlight on people like us even brighter than it was after Oregon. Tonight, was supposed to be a statement of strength and resolve. Instead...well, you showed up." Seventy-Two forcefully lifted Dante from the ground and stood him up.

"It must be obvious to you by now that since I've got you, I must also know where your little girlfriend and her family are, too. Well, you're right. I followed you from downtown, but you were too blind to notice that you were being followed. This is chess, not checkers, son," Seventy-Two said, his voice booming with disdain toward Dante. "But don't worry. I'm not going to hurt those you love just to get to you. That's too cliché. I'm just going to hurt you. That's the type of 'bad guy' I am."

Instead of feeding into the monologue that was being delivered, Dante reacted by swinging his right fist toward Seventy-Two with such force that the Jeep to their right shook and raised slightly from the ground. Just as quickly as Dante swung, Seventy-Two ducked and struck Dante in the stomach with a blow that sent him flying about twenty yards back. Hovering above the ground, Seventy-Two stared down at Dante, who was gathering himself.

"Consider this my warning shot. I will not veer from my mission. There is still much to be done. My enemies will pay for what they did to me and the others." Seventy-Two said as he refused to break his intense gaze from Dante's eyes. "You have ensured your inclusion in the long line of those who I will come for and end. Tonight is not the night for you, young man. But your time is coming," Seventy-Two declared as he thrust himself into the night sky and flew off into the distance.

Chapter Eight

Following his encounter with Dante, Seventy-Two returned to a small abandoned warehouse which was the lone building on a plot of land located on the outskirts of town. He chose this area because it was secluded enough thanks to the wooded area around the building. This warehouse would serve as the location which allowed him to refocus his energy and form the strategy for what he called his "reclamation project."

What bothered Seventy-Two to his core now was Dante. He had not expected to come across any other Specials, let alone a kid with the audacity to try standing between him and his plan of action. But now he had to deal with this obstruction; he just wasn't sure exactly how. Thoughts of terminating the intrusive individual mixed with other thoughts of training the young man up to fight alongside him.

Pacing back and forth in the darkness of the warehouse, Seventy-Two rubbed his right hand from his forehead down to his chin, tracing a long-since scarred wound from his battles with his captors. "You can't let him in, man. He'll only distract you from what you're trying to accomplish," he said as he shook his head from left to right before continuing on. "Yeah... but he might prove valuable. Having another warrior of our ilk could in fact move us closer to finishing what we've started."

Seventy-Two was wrought with conflict as he continued to walk around the wide open second floor. "He crossed the line, you fool! You know what must be done. How dare you second guess yourself. There is no time to waste on this insignificant interruption. He should have been finished tonight! It's too early to be making mistakes like this. NO MORE! You...I know what must be done now." Seventy-Two continued rambling then suddenly stopped his pacing. Quickly and violently he swung his right arm out and shot a beam of light to the wall on the opposite side of the room.

The impact of the energy blast resulted in concrete and mortar being shot into the air. It was in this moment that he closed his eyes, reached out with both his hands and stopped

the concrete from going any farther. Realizing what he had

just done, Seventy-Two began to move his hands at a faster

rate of speed, and he witnessed the bricks and other pieces

that flew from the wall being placed back, just as they were.

"This might come in handy," he said as he pulled his mask

back on.

Dante could not believe what had just happened over

the last several hours. The night had started off with an

enjoyable date with Martha, but quickly spiraled out of

control. He'd exposed his powers to the public, barely

managed to keep his identity hidden, and had a second

encounter with the individual who had just caused a

catastrophic amount of destruction.

Perched atop a building, he gazed off into the distance.

Realizing that he must look like some character from a comic,

he quickly stepped down from the ledge and shook off the

awkward feeling of being a walking copy and paste superhero

stereotype. "Yuck," he muttered quietly as he attempted to

gather himself. At this point in his life, he knew he was still essentially a kid. A kid who had seen tremendous adversity through the years and a kid who now found himself in the middle of a war, but still completely inexperienced.

"The first question," he said, "is what the hell is this war about? The second is, what's my part in all this?"

Almost instantaneously he came to terms with his gifts and abilities and felt at peace with the realization of what his place in this world was. Dante leapt into the sky and flew amongst the stars. Swerving in and out of the clouds, Dante looked down on the city he had called his home for so long and increased his speed until he felt dizzy and laughed out loud. He crossed county lines first, then state lines. Minutes had passed before he realized just how far he had traveled. In a short amount of time, he had flown from California to Colorado. As he let that sink in, he realized that in just about the same amount of time, he could go from Colorado to Oregon...where the initial attack took place.

As he arrived in the Clatsop State Forest, he was overcome with a feeling of dread and despair. He reduced the altitude that he was flying at and allowed himself to be concealed by the treetops. Following the attack, Dante had conducted plenty of research on what had happened in the compound and the surrounding area. Since the attack, there was nothing. It was almost as if the government wanted to erase all public memory and evidence of the compound. He continued on when, off in the distance, he noticed two sets of headlights, sitting stationary on the outside of a fence.

He brought himself to rest on a tree branch about sixty feet above the ground. Dante continued to observe the area and noticed that there was plenty of activity on the opposite side of the fence which was being guarded by two military vehicles. This compound had not been shut down following the attack as was reported on local and national news. Whatever was going on before was still going on. "What the hell?" he said as he noticed a rapidly approaching projectile coming in his direction. Instinctively, Dante jumped from the branch, but was seconds too late. The surface-to-air missile struck the tree and caused it to fall on top of him.

The vehicles that were parked on the outside of the fence about two-hundred yards away began to make their way toward the impact site. Floating in and out of consciousness, Dante tried to pick himself up from the ground. He managed to lift his head enough to see that there was a bit of separation between the vehicles, that caused by the trees. In survival mode, he reached down and grabbed one of the massive tree limbs that had fallen to the ground, spun around, and launched it at the vehicle on his right. The tree limb struck the ground with enough force that it stood straight up, and the incoming vehicle slammed directly into it and halted immediately while the driver was ejected through the windshield and into the darkness.

As the other vehicle continued to barrel onward, Dante accepted that the impact was inevitable. The headlights were getting brighter now. Just as the vehicle began to open fire,

Dante fell backwards, allowing himself to land flat on the ground and the vehicle drove directly over top of him. In the seconds that followed, Dante reached up and grabbed the bumper. Standing up slowly, he lifted the vehicle above the ground and shook it violently, causing the driver to fall out and hit the ground with a sickening thud.

Dante took several paces toward the man, who was nervously trying to reach his firearm. "Really? You fired a missile at me and think that a pistol is going to be more effective?" Dante said smiling. He kicked the gun from the man's hand, reached down and grabbed a hold of his vest, and lifted him into the air. "I think you might have some information for me, right?" Dante said as the man nodded in agreement.

Chapter Nine

"You did what?!?" Scott blurted out as he stood up quickly from his bed where he had several textbooks scattered about. Dante had just spent the last few minutes detailing his romantic and heroic escapades to his long-time best friend. Not a moment was left out of the account that Dante delivered to Scott...everything from his dinner with Martha to his flying to Oregon to visit the site of the attack months before.

The funny thing about Scott's reaction to this news was that he knew full well what Dante was capable of. He'd known about the super abilities that his friend was gifted with, but had sworn to keep everything to himself, even after his mother was killed. Now, it seemed

Dante may have just paid a visit to those very people. "Bro! What the hell? I can't even..." Scott said as he stopped himself and leaned onto the dresser at the other side of the room. Looking up into the mirror in front of him, his eyes made a glancing connection with Dante's.

Signaling for his friend to calm down, Dante inhaled and attempted to compose himself before continuing his recounting.

"I'm sure you have questions and you might even be mad at me for doing what I did. No one was hurt in Oregon tonight. I went in for a reconnaissance mission and got the information I was looking for," he explained.

"Yeah, man, I guess you're right…all of that makes total sense. Except for the part where YOU went on a reconnaissance mission! What is that all about? Why would you involve yourself in something like this? This is clearly way out of your league, and you just interjected yourself without really thinking about the consequences. But, hey…you gathered information, right? What'd you get?" Scott continued, almost glowing with anger as he glared at Dante.

"I know that the guy who led the attack downtown tonight has a codename. He was called Seventy-Two; he was gathered by this semi-secret government organization that was tasked to find people with special abilities, like way outside of a typical human's abilities. Wingard, one of the guys who was killed in the attack, went off the rails and began experimenting on these people. He used inhumane tactics to collect 'Specials' as the government refers to them. Anyway, he poked and prodded them to no end. That's apparently what pushed Seventy-Two to take actions and cause the trouble last night," Dante said as he sat down at Scott's desk.

"Do you understand how crazy this all sounds…and, quite frankly, how crazy it all is? You referred to them as 'these people'. Dante, YOU are one of those people! You're on the radar now and I don't think you could care any less. I could be on their radar…. Shit man, Martha could be on their radar! I'm having a tough time wrapping my head around the madness you just slammed down at my feet."

Dante spun around in the computer chair and glanced down at the additional pile of books that were strewn about on Scott's desk, and Scott hurried over and gathered them and his notebooks. "So, are you just going to ignore the fact that I went on another date with Martha? Can you at least acknowledge that part of the night with some semblance of positivity?" Dante said, smiling.

Looking down at his feet, Scott could not fight the grin that crept onto his face. "Alright man, way to go," he said as he leaned in for an uncomfortably awkward handshake hug combination.

"Yeah, maybe we skip the hug next time, yeah?" Dante said as Scott shot him a thumbs up in response. "So, you said they called him 'Seventy-Two.' Does that mean there are more?" Scott asked.

"I scanned the place and didn't see signs of an abundance of other 'prisoners' there. But that doesn't mean that there weren't others who were taken somewhere else following the attack," Dante replied. "You scanned the place? Does that mean you have x-ray vision too?" Scott asked with a tone of astonishment in his voice.

"Yep. You can add x-ray vision to the list of abilities that this thrift store Superman has," Dante said laughing.

Immediately following his response, Dante squinted his eyes very tightly and looked towards Scott.

"Not funny dude! Not funny!" Scott said as he crossed his arms below his waist. "So, what do we do now?" he asked.

"We? Are you saying that you want in on whatever this is?" Dante asked quizzically.

"Well yeah. You're not the only one with powers," Scott replied as he disappeared from sight.

Dante looked around the room quickly, but was unable to locate his friend. *SMACK*! Dante lifted his hand to his forehead, which was just thumped unexpectedly. "Scott? what are you doing?" he asked as he was pushed to the floor by a force he could not see. Landing on Scott's bed, Dante looked toward the direction he was pushed from, and slowly, Scott began to reappear.

"So yeah, I want in. Let's do some good. Superhero high-five!" Scott said as he leapt into the air and was pleased when his hand was met by Dante's in superhero high-five unity. When this strange dynamic duo came back down to the ground, their eyes shifted to the bedroom doorway where Martha stood.

"Really guys? High-fives? You're seemingly on the cusp of a battle that will be talked about for years to come and you go for a high-five. Classy," she said as she crossed the threshold and stepped into the room.

The three smiled together as Dante's eyes locked on Martha's. At that moment, he knew, that in the years to come, he would still talk about how he could get lost in her hazel eyes. As she approached, Dante lifted his hand into the air. With a puzzled look on her face, Martha looked toward Scott, who had just lifted his left hand into the air and stopped it just short of where Dante's hand was. It was in this moment that Martha knew that not only was she dating one of the two goofiest people on the planet, but that Dante knew she had fallen in love. Martha raised her hand and completed the high-five trifecta.

"Yes! So, what powers do you have?" Scott asked Martha excitedly and with a schoolgirl type giddiness in his voice.

"Well, it appears that I have just discovered that I have the ability to withstand a ridiculous high-five scenario. That counts for something, right?"

Dante moved in quickly for a hug that seemed to freeze time. In that moment, he felt as if only he and Martha existed and that nothing else mattered.

Interrupting the moment, as he typically did with an effortless skill, Scott blurted out, "Alright! I dub thee, High-Five Girl."

Shaking her head and grabbing onto Dante's hand, Martha sighed deeply. "Okay, Scott. But if you say that in front of anyone else but us three…" she trailed off as Scott gestured that he was zipping his lips. The three friends were quiet the. Unsure of what to do next, and certainly unable to fathom what would come down the line, they stood united and determined to make a difference from this moment and

beyond.

Chapter Ten

Following the brutal attack downtown

, the public was understandably bothered by the lack

of information being released by local government officials

and law enforcement agencies. Left to their own devices,

people will create tales and narratives that feed into the

paranoia and fear that undoubtedly arises following events of

the courthouse disaster magnitude.

Amid increasing pressure, mayor James Dixon, who'd

found himself at the center of the attack that brought the city

to a screeching halt scheduled a press conference to take

place nearly two weeks afterwards.

The delay was a result of the mayor and his cabinet

scurrying to gather information that was not made available

to them by the officials that ranked higher than they did. For

the first ten days that followed the attack, groups of

protesters gathered outside of his office and home. For the

most part, the gatherings were peaceful, but there was the

occasional protester who was arrested for becoming disorderly.

The press conference was a heavily guarded event that included military personnel who were staged behind metal barricades set up on a perimeter encircling the mayor's podium.

In addition to the security that was set up on the grounds near the stage, snipers were placed on rooftops surrounding the courthouse in the event of an approaching threat.

Mayor Dixon sat alone, nervously, in an office within the courthouse. Reaching into his jacket pocket, he removed a handkerchief and dabbed his freshly powdered face to remove the sweat from his forehead. Utilizing breathing techniques that he had been taught to help deal with the anxiety he'd developed as a result of the attack, he found himself feeling as though he would pass out at any second. A knock came to the door, and was followed by an abrupt: "Five minutes, Mr. Mayor!"

Dixon stood up from his chair and ran his hands down the front of his navy-blue suit. He then reached up to his crimson-red tie and straightened it prior to dabbing the sweat from his face again. The he knelt down to say a prayer. Just as he was finishing, the door opened and a guard who was holding a high-capacity assault rifle poked his head in to the room.

"Are you ready, sir?" he asked. Mayor Dixon stood up and nodded his head as he made his way to the doorway.

Flanked by two guards in front and behind him, the mayor and his entourage walked down the hall to the stairway that would lead them to their destination. As the mayor ascended the stairs and peered out from the curtain which was hung at the opening of the doorway, he couldn't help but be overcome by a feeling of déjà vu. It had been just two short weeks ago that he'd made a similar walk to a podium where fire and death had followed.

Gazing out at the crowd that gathered beyond the guardrails, which were protected by heavily armed military personnel, Mayor Dixon felt slightly better than he did the last time he'd made an address to the public. One major difference this time was that he was not speaking to a crowd of supporters, but a crowd that demanded answers and the reassurance of their safety. Here, he was their leader, not a candidate. The mayor took note of the teleprompter that stood at the base of the podium.

The guard who led the escort team looked toward the mayor and nodded his head, indicating that it was time for the Mayor to address the public. Nervously, the mayor saluted the guard and made his way through the curtain, stopping at the podium. He lifted his head slowly from the papers in front of him and glanced across the crowd. He recognized people he had seen at his rallies in the past, but most were not familiar. These people had fear in their eyes and were looking for assurance and direction from their mayor.

"Ladies and gentlemen, thank you for joining me today," the mayor began as he adjusted the glasses on his face. "Nearly two weeks ago, our fair city was attacked by beings who are not like you or I. These individuals possess abilities which could, and did, prove disastrous to our citizenry. The government facility in Oregon was clearly only the first target of a group of "Specials" who look to cause damage, death, and destruction throughout this nation." He cleared his throat and steadied his trembling hands.

"But I implore you. Do not allow these Specials to affect your daily lives. Instead, be vigilant. If you see something that is abnormal, say something; inform your local law enforcement agency. Immediately. These Specials are clearly here to bring pain and anguish. I will not stand for it. That is why at this very moment, I am signing a declaration of war on any Special who dares to show their face to the public. The faces you see behind me on the screens are the individuals who are directly responsible for the destruction that occurred here two weeks ago."

The images on the screen included Seventy-Two, the two beings who traveled with him, and Dante. "If you see these individuals, do not engage them. I have authorized a military presence throughout the city that has been given the authority to strike against these Specials. You need not spend another second worrying about your safety. We will protect you." Mayor Dixon raised both of his arms and he was quickly flanked by additional heavily armed guards. "Now, does anyone have any questions?" the mayor asked as a guard approached him from behind.

Stopping just inches behind the mayor, the guard removed his helmet and tapped the mayor's shoulder. "I have one for you, Mr. Mayor," Seventy-Two said as he grasped Dixon's shirt and lifted him into the air. "Who is going to save you now?" he asked as he spun the mayor and slammed him head first into the pavement.

The crowd began screaming and scattering, and several flocked toward the military guards who were perched at the barricades. Grabbing the microphone from the stand on the podium, Seventy-Two removed the military garb he was dressed in and revealed a black armored suit with a purple, glowing "72" on the right chest plate. He then lifted his head and glared out toward the crowd.

"Ladies and gentlemen of this fair city. I am known as Seventy-Two. I am one of the Specials that your beloved mayor had spoken so lovingly. I am here to tell you that you are safe for now. My mission is much larger than causing petty destruction and vandalism. Just know, that I am not alone, and I will show force as I see fit. I am not here to hurt any of you today. But know that I will come back if I need to." He said as he changed his focus from the crowd to the camera. "And I will be back for you, boy," he said as he squinted his eyes which were visible through the eyeholes in his mask as he threw the microphone at the camera, ending the live news feed.

Chapter Eleven

After Seventy-Two's brazen attack and the assassination of the mayor, numerous demonstrations occurred across the country. Fear and anger had gripped the nation after the events in Oregon, and had only tightened its stranglehold over the population after the events in Los Angeles. The demonstrations that popped up were a mixture of Anti-Special and Seventy-Two sympathizers... there was no in-between. The news networks tried covering this developing story objectively, but many ultimately reverted to the primal reaction of anger and fear, due to what they could not understand.

The Anti-Special demonstrators were a mixture of peaceful and aggressive groups which gathered at national landmarks in order to get the most attention from the networks. From Seattle to Newark, the major news networks highlighted the cities who played host to the most violent protests. Overturned cars, heavily armed and armored riot police, and darkened evening skylines which were occasionally illuminated by the fires that burned in the cities below. Hatred flowed as fluidly as water in the uncertain climate that had been created by the introduction of real, super-powered individuals who had the ability to cause mass destruction with the snap of a finger.

Amidst the violence that was unfolding from state to state, the President of the United States made his stance clear to the nation. Calling for the congress to come together to form an official plan of action including the incarceration or exile of these individuals who, in his eyes, "Stand against the very fabric of America and what Her citizens stand for."

In Baltimore, Maryland, the president held an impromptu press conference to address the growing concerns and increasing violence that was plaguing the nation. As the president walked up to the podium, he was greeted by a massive crowd that represented the divide that ran through the population.

"My fellow Americans," he began, "we find ourselves in a challenging time. A very challenging time, indeed. We have never faced a threat such as the one that is at our doorstep at this very moment. Violent individuals of superior powers and capabilities have risen to our awareness and have left many of us and our communities in tatters. A military facility has been attacked, a mayor assassinated, and God only knows what is to come next." The president paused as he attempted to gather his thoughts. Inhaling deeply and adjusting his bright red tie, he looked out to the crowd.

"This country stands on a foundation of strength and truth, and by God, that foundation will not be shaken. Stand firm in the understanding that we will not be phased by the attacks of a line of individuals who oppose the very spirit of our great nation. We have faced adversity in the past and will again in the future. This cannot and will not define us," the President concluded. As he stepped back from the microphone, he raised both hands into the air, acknowledging the applause coming from the crowd.

As the president turned his back to the crowd, Dante made his presence known as he pushed several onlookers aside gently. As he stepped into an opening, he levitated above the crowd and folded his arms across his chest.

"Excuse me, Mr. President!" Dante shouted as the onlookers shifted their attention from the president to the Special hovering above them. "I was there after Oregon. I have come face-to-face with Seventy-Two on several occasions. I do not accept the generalization that has been created and supported by you, the leader of the free world. I am not what you say; not all Specials are violent terrorists. I stand for the very values that you claim to hold dear. I stand for truth, justice, and the American way." With this, a spattering of applause arose from the crowd.

"You're not Superman!" shouted one of the onlookers.

"I am well aware of that, and I don't claim to be. I didn't ask for this, but rest assured, I will stand with you as we battle this threat together" Dante said as he lowered himself back to the ground.

The tension that was in the air prior to the president's address seemed to be fading away. The crowd began to split, opening up a clear path as Dante began walking towards the stage where the president still stood. The guards standing at the President's side unholstered their weapons and raised them, aiming them at Dante. The president lifted his arms and gently put his hands atop the weapons, signaling for his guards to lower them. He seemed unafraid of the approaching Special as he motioned for the guards to step back from the stage.

The crowd began to buzz with anticipation as Dante left the ground and flew up to the stage, stopping on the opposite side of the podium that separated him from the president. "Mr. President, I am willing to look past the terrible things that you have said about people like me. I am willing to fight for this nation and protect the population from the threat of Seventy-Two or any other evil that it may face. But we have to show that we are stronger than the divide between us. Sure, we're different. That's plain to see. But that does not make me a threat. We all have different abilities. It is what you do with those abilities, how you choose to act, that will determine our relationship moving forward," Dante said as he stepped around the podium and stood side by side with the president.

The president locked his eyes on Dante, silently pondering what to do or say next. He found himself in a situation very different than he had anticipated when he took the stage. A crowd that was once so powerfully divided had now seem to come together as one...and for some reason, the president was unsure of how to react to this development. The hate and fear subsided, even in the face of one of the Specials, but the President found himself unable to make the next move. Noticing this, Dante reached out his right hand and fixed his eyes on the presidents'. Instinctively, the president went to shake Dante's hand, but he quickly pulled his hand back. A gentle rumble began to rise from the crowd.

Dante did not move his hand from the position he had put it in. He flashed a smile and motioned his head to his right hand, attempting to let the president know that he wanted to join his fight, and that everything would be fine. Finally, the president smiled, reached out his right hand, and grabbed on to Dante's. The two shook hands and the crowd of onlookers erupted in a wave of applause and adulation.

"My fellow Americans, it is on this day that I am proud to say that we stand for a nation that is undivided. We are a land of acceptance, always have been and always should be. Let us not allow the actions of a few bad apples to dictate how we act towards each other. Instead, let's come together and continue to grow as the strong country that we are. Today, this young man has demonstrated a strength and resolve that is uncommon in much of society. I challenge you to follow the example of this exceptional being and we will triumph over the evil that has befallen this great nation. What's your name, young man?" the president concluded.

With a beaming smile, Dante nodded towards the President and shifted his gaze out to the crowd. "I'm Dante," he proclaimed with a deeper voice than he had been speaking with as the crowd reacted positively.

"You're not Batman!" shouted another onlooker.

"Yeah, I know," Dante said as he lowered his head, shook it, and let out a faint laugh.

Chapter Twelve

Surprisingly, there was minimal fallout from Dante's revelation to the nation that there were more Specials than just Seventy-Two and the duo he occasionally surrounded himself with. Dante knew of the risk that came along with going public and exposing himself, which is why he initially covered his face with his tattered shirt during his first encounter with Seventy-Two. However, with the political and social climate in the country being as volatile as it was, Dante felt that he had no other choice.

Back at home, Dante's decision rocked his neighborhood and the surrounding communities. Scott and Steve were working a closing shift at the diner when Dante spoke to the crowd in Maryland. Camera crews were at the president's rally and his address was being broadcast on national and local news programs. Scott was taking a tray of food to one of the tables he was waiting on when Dante delivered his "I'm Dante" line and Steve was working in the kitchen with the televisions out of his view, but he was able to distinguish his friends' voice.

"Hey, doesn't that guy work here?" said a restaurant patron as Scott was putting the glasses on the table. The guest looked away from the television and addressed Scott more directly. "I asked you a question...doesn't that freak work here?" he said as the anger within him increased with each syllable that exited his mouth.

"Yeah, you know what...he does work here. But I'm really... really close to not working here if you keep..." Scott said as Steve appeared seemingly out of nowhere to redirect his friend to the kitchen. Begrudgingly, Scott made his way to the swinging door behind the counter, pushed it open, and disappeared from sight.

Looking over his shoulder to make sure that Scott was indeed in the kitchen, Steve switched his focus to the guests at the table. Wiping his forehead with the back of his right forearm, Steve addressed the guests. "Man, that got awkward pretty quickly, huh? This should go without saying, but you folks are no longer welcome here. In fact, why don't you just take your meal to go?" he said as he began to back away from the table.

"Yeah, but we ain't done here yet," said one of the men at the table.

"No, I think you are," Steve replied as Scott emerged from the kitchen with two to-go bags in his hands. Steve walked over to Scott and grabbed the bags from his friend. "You upset because I called him what he really is? A freak. I call 'em like I see 'em. This is America, right?" the man continued. It was with this sentence that the atmosphere in the room changed drastically.

Standing directly in front of the bar counter, Scott looked at the men who were now standing up from the table they were previously seated at. "Yeah, and I'm telling you to leave this restaurant," Scott said, pointing his finger quickly at the door. The four men appeared to be at an impasse, and, realizing this, Scott opened his outstretched hand and the door flew open violently, hitting the back of the

99

seat of the booth behind it, shattering the glass of the door on impact.

"Yeah, we'll take that to go," the man said as he and his companions grabbed their bags and quickly shuffled to the door. As they exited the restaurant, they unknowingly ran past Dante, who had just landed, literally descended from the sky in the parking lot from his flight back from Maryland.

"What's their hurry?" Dante said as he stepped into the restaurant. He looked around, observing the news was airing coverage of his grand debut, and made his way to the middle barstool.

"We decided to close a little early," Scott replied as he signaled for Steve to come over from the table that he had found himself frozen at with both arms extended as if they were still holding the to-go bags.

"What's up, discount store Batman?!?" shouted Steve as he snapped back to reality. Being used to Steve's quips, Dante smiled and shrugged the statement off. He sat down, grabbed the remote control from the counter in front of him, and switched the television off.

Almost as if he knew what Dante would ask for, Scott made a strawberry milkshake and handed it over to his friend.

Dante smiled, recognizing the significance of the strawberry milkshake. The night of Scott's mom's death, the two had escaped then been united with the police officers who were taking care of the young boys following the tragic events that befell them. One officer brought both Scott and Dante a strawberry milkshake. "Let them be kids while they are still able," the officer had said to his partner, who was staring a hole right through him. Holding their milkshakes tightly, both boys put one arm around the other as they took their sips through red striped straws.

"So, should we expect an invite to the White House? You know, since you and the Prez are so tight now. I'm gonna have to go buy a suit or something, I don't have anything fancy enough for an event like that," Steve said.

"We're not getting an invite. After we walked off the stage, he told me that he appreciated my honesty, but wanted to let me know that I... and people like me... would not be above the law. He said that there have to be checks and balances. He made it very clear that, while he respects what makes us different, we will not be friends. And to be completely honest with you, I'm okay with that. I'm at peace with what I did today. I tried show the world and Specials like me that we are not all evil and we don't have to remain in hiding," Dante said as he paused to take a sip of his milkshake which immediately caused a smile to break across his face.

"I mean, let's be real here, this is an unprecedented opportunity," he said.

"Hell yeah! With you and Scott leading the way, this could be a revolution. The beginning of a new era in this country. Picture it, Dante and Scott...or Scott and Dante, depending on how you guys want to be introduced... with their manager/agent Steve. The possibilities are endless." said Steve.

The three shared a laugh, which was quickly interrupted by the front window of the diner being smashed by a brick and the screeching of tires outside. Steve and Scott ducked down, unsure of what could come next, but Dante sprang up from his barstool and flew through the opening in the window following the direction of the speeding car.

Dante stayed high enough from the ground to get a clear look at the road ahead of him as the car drove erratically through traffic, switching lanes and cutting off other vehicles on the road. Looking about two blocks ahead, Dante saw a mother walking in the crosswalk holding hands with her daughter. The thought of the car plowing through the crosswalk and sending the mother and daughter careening through the air gave Dante chills and made him hurry.

Crossing the street, the little girl dropped her pink, stuffed teddy bear and let go of her mother's hand to go back and get it. Barreling forward in excess of one-hundred miles per hour, the car swerved into oncoming traffic and then back into the correct lane. The little girl picked up her teddy bear and in an instant, Dante swooped down in front of her and slammed both of his hands on the hood of the oncoming car, sending the driver crashing through the windshield and into the air.

The instant he realized that the car had come to a complete stop and the little girl was safe, he reached out his left hand and caught the man by the collar of his jacket in mid-air. A crowd of bystanders gathered and looked on in awe at what they had just seen. The mother, who had collapsed to the ground in fear, stood up and ran to her daughter, picking her up and hugging her tightly.

"You're… you're… " the woman struggled as she tried to get words out. "Thank you, Dante. Thank you," she said as she reached over and pulled him in for an embrace. When the mother hugged Dante while holding her daughter, the crowd buzzed and then burst into applause, chanting his name. "Dante, Dante, Dante!"

Chapter Thirteen

In the Summer of 2021, two years removed from Dante's emergence as the second publicly known Special following Seventy-Two, the landscape of Dante's life began to shift dramatically. Dante found himself at the beginning of real superhero lore. While his powers reflected those which were on display in comic books published over the span of decades, he, Scott, and Seventy-Two found themselves at the center of a controversial subject that had not previously been broached in human history.

Despite all the notoriety, the interview requests, television appearances, and heroic feats, Dante and Martha's relationship grew as the two spent more time together.

"She's the one, man," Dante said smiling as he and Scott sat on the edge of the roof of Scott's apartment building.

With a look on his face that Dante had seen countless times over the years, Scott shifted his gaze to the expansive skyline before them. "You've been saying that. Pretty sure you've been saying that since the first night at the diner," he said shaking his head. "When are you going to do something about it?"

Nodding his head, Dante reached into his pocket and pulled out black velvet ring box. At the sight of this, Scott's eyes lit up and he quickly reached over to snatch the box out of his friend's hand. From where he was sitting, Dante could see the reflection of the ring in Scott's eyes as he gently picked it up and pulled it closer to his face. "So, I guess now?" Scott said.

"Yeah, now. I've been saving up for the last six months and have just been trying to figure out how I would ask, you know?" Dante said.

"I got you... first, you and Martha go out for a romantic dinner or whatever you romantics do. Then, you come home and sit up here... like you and I are doing right now. After a few minutes of taking this beautiful sight in, you ask her to stand up and when she does, you both go into the air... slowly, allowing her to take in everything around her. After you guys get your lovey-dovey moment over with, you land back on the edge. It's at this moment that I, using my invisibility powers, appear just to put the box in her hand right before I disappear again. She's all Brad Pitt like... 'What's in the box!?!' and she opens it. BOOM! Problem solved!" Scott drew a deep breath, having delivered his speech in one breath and was now winded.

Rubbing his hand back and forth on his chin, Dante looked toward the sky as he imagined the scenario playing out. "Yeah, man. That's not bad. But why do you have to be there?" he said as he shoved his friend gently and began laughing.

"Why do... me... pssssh... the nerve!" Scott said as he suddenly began struggling to form a cohesive sentence.

"For real, though, what should I wear when I'm handing her the box?" Scott said as the two simultaneously burst into laughter.

That Friday evening, Dante made arrangements to meet with Martha at a relatively new upscale Mexican restaurant downtown. They had been dating consistently for some time now, so this evening did not seem much different than any of their recent ones, which was the effect Dante was going for. He didn't want to do anything out of the norm, but he chose a new restaurant in an attempt at keeping her unaware.

After their meal, they drove back to Dante's apartment building and parked outside. As the sun was setting, the two carried on a conversation for almost an hour before the sun was out of sight and the darkness of the sky was sprinkled with stars spread as far as the eye could see.

Their conversation spanned the normal topics, the danger of what Dante did, who he had saved lately, and did he feel pain? Then turned to how Martha's studies were going. Dante exited the vehicle, walked over to the passenger side, and opened the door with his right hand, outstretching his left. Looking up at him with a gleam in her eye and a slight smile on her face, Martha reached her right hand out and placed it in Dante's.

As she stood up in front of him, she wrapped her arms around his waist and lay her head on his chest like she had done numerous times in the past. "I can hear your heart beating," she said. "It proves to me that you're not that much different from me after all."

Dante made sure that Martha's arms were wrapped tightly enough around him and then he ascended into the night sky, bypassing the roof and climbing to a point that was just high enough that they could both see over the entire city. Martha had witnessed and even had experienced Dante's gifts firsthand, but this had felt different to her. There seemed to be more to this than their previous flights.

The two hovered amongst the clouds and closer to the stars than they had ever been and held on tightly to each other as they observed the sight of street lights, illuminated skyscrapers, and passing airplanes. Martha hadn't stopped smiling since she took Dante's hand prior to exiting the car. Seeing this cemented the feeling that Dante had in his heart that this woman was the one he would spend the rest of his life with.

Dante descended to the ledge of the rooftop on his apartment building. Taking a deep breath, he nodded his head and suddenly Scott appeared as planned, dressed in a pin striped suit and red tie, and handed Martha the black velvet box before disappearing again.

"*What?!*" Martha said, unable to move her eyes from the box, until she saw Dante on bended knee in front of her.

"Martha, you are the sky that holds the stars, and you are the sunshine that brightens an ever-darkening world. You are the anchor to my constantly rocking boat, and you are the woman I cannot imagining living without. I've felt this way from the moment I laid eyes on you, and that feeling has only strengthened over time. Will you marry me?"

Nodding her head up and down and with tears streaming from her eyes, Dante slid the ring onto her finger.

Overcome with joy, Martha knelt down and wrapped her arms around Dante as tightly as she could. "Yes. A million times, yes!" she said as the two held onto one another for another moment.

"Scott, get back out here." Martha said as she and Dante stood up. Off in the distance, Scott reappeared and began to slowly move toward the couple. Dante and Martha held hands as they turned to Scott, who looked like he was having difficulty finding words to convey what he was feeling.

"I'm so happy for both of you. I truly am. Dante, we've been friends since we were little and now, here I stand, watching you as you propose to one of the most wonderful women I've ever known," he said, blushing.

Scott fought back tears as images of his and Dante's past ran through his mind. Images of the two of them playing together in elementary school, of them in Scott's parents' house, and the memories of the two as they began to discover who they were in the world, together and as individuals.

Scott placed his left hand on Dante's shoulder and his right hand on Martha's as he lowered his head and took another deep breath. "I've prayed for the day that you would find happiness. Hell, I've prayed that we could all find happiness. It's been a rocky road that led you to this moment, and I know that you truly have found contentment. I can see it in your eyes when you speak about Martha. I can see it in her eyes when she speaks about you. And because of that, I can rest easy knowing that my prayers have been heard." Scott wiped away a lone tear from his cheek.

"You sappy SOB," Dante said as he reached out and brought Scott in for a hug.

As she looked at Dante and Scott holding onto each other, Martha rocked back and forth on her heels, waiting patiently for her chance to chime in. Dante and Scott relinquished their hold on each other and Dante moved closer to Martha. Wrapping her right arm around his waist, Martha looked toward Scott and winked. "Do you have anything else you need to say, Scott?" she asked.

Scott placed both hands in his pants pockets and paced for a brief moment before leaning in close to Dante's left ear. "You're going to be a father," he said quietly.

Dante staggered backwards for a moment before he regained his balance. Unable to speak and overcome with emotion, Dante looked into Martha's eyes and without hesitation she said, "Yeah, that's right, Slugger. We're going to be parents."

Chapter Fourteen

March 3, 2022, New York City. Perched at the top of the Empire State Building, Seventy-Two looked out over the snow-covered city. With the wind whipping around him and the snow settling atop his shoulders, Seventy-Two stared off as he contemplated his next course of action. He had decided to lay low, doing his best to stay off the grid since the events in Oregon and the assassination of the mayor, but he hadn't been inactive in the time that had lapsed.

"This is chess, not checkers," he would remind himself as he toiled over a painstakingly detailed planning process, alone in the abandoned warehouse in Los Angeles. *Chess, not checkers.* Which meant that his first moves had only been a test of his opponent's defenses. His real attacks were yet to come, and he would not rest until he carried out every step of his Reclamation Project.

The snow continued to pile on the ground below him and the rush hour traffic had come to a halt; Seventy-Two's eyes widened as he saw the opportunity that he had been waiting for. In the past nine months, Dante had propelled into a star-level status. The more Dante helped put out fires, rescue stranded passengers on cruise ships, and reduce gang violence in what was a city known for such violence for decades, the more people forgot about the military facility in Oregon. That meant that they would forget Seventy-Two's plight and the nightmare he had managed to pull himself out of. And, ultimately, they would forget about him.

The streets below him were reflecting red from the brake lights halted due to the increasing accumulation of snow. He pulled a mask over his mouth and brushed off the soft snow that had piled on his shoulders. Standing above the city, almost lost in the falling snow, and just barely visible by the glowing purple seventy-two on his chest plate, Seventy-Two lifted his mask and fixed it onto his face as he took a step forward and began to descend rapidly, headfirst from one-hundred stories above the city.

As he plummeted toward the ground, people still inside the Empire State Building saw him as he cut through the darkening sky at an increasing rate of speed. Those who were in the building grew more concerned by the second. "That couldn't have been *him*, right?" said one of the men inside the conference room on the eighty-third floor. "He's usually on the west coast... he wouldn't have come all the way over here." While the man continued his attempts at rationalizing what he may have just seen, one of his coworkers peered out the window and down toward the streets.

As he began to close in on the streets below him, Seventy-Two leveled himself off, reduced his speed, and was now horizontal with the ground. Hovering there, he allowed enough time for some of the civilians to see him and in an instant, he was joined by his cohorts who wore matching armor-plated gear. The three remained elevated, approximately twenty feet above the ground, and as more people saw them, they began to exit their vehicles and run through the mounting snow and crowds of pedestrians who were fleeing.

Seventy-Two turned his head to look at the individuals to his side, and, with a silent approval, he nodded toward the cars. The two flew in separate directions and swooped downward toward the vehicles. Simultaneously, they lifted cars in rapid succession and lofted them into the air above. As the cars rose into the sky, Seventy-Two blasted energy beams at them. And as the beams struck the vehicles, they were instantly eradicated.

Within minutes, the trio caused a massive number of casualties, but there was no police presence as a result of the difficulty navigating through the deteriorating road conditions. News of the attack began to spread as several people who'd made it to safety were able to capture footage on their cellphones. Social media aided in spreading the news of this horrific attack, dispersing it to the rest of the world. As quickly as information moved electronically, Dante was made aware of what was occurring in New York City via text from Scott.

Scott did not want to bother Dante. In fact, he had spent the last couple of weeks making a conscious effort to let the newlyweds… and new parents have time to themselves. Scott had stepped up as his powers had expanded to include strength far superior to that of any other human. Dante, Martha, and their baby daughter, Bethany, had been home for just eight days before his phone lit up with text messages from his close friend.

"NYC…Seventy-Two is attacking NYC!" read one text message from Scott.

Martha glanced over and saw the phone light up and caught a quick glimpse of the message. Holding Bethany, she got up out of her chair and walked over to Dante, who seemed to be having a difficult time figuring out what to do. "Honey. We'll be fine. I think you know what you need to do," Martha told him as she placed Bethany in the swing in the corner of their bedroom.

Reaching into their closet, she grabbed a hanger that held a covered article of clothing. She took several steps from the closet to stand behind Dante as he looked out their window and placed her hand on his shoulder. The past few months had been relatively quiet for the couple, with the exception of preparing for the baby's arrival. Their wedding ceremony was low-key, which is something that Dante and Martha both wanted, especially with the rise of Dante's status as a hero in the eyes of the public.

Dante raised his head and turned to face his wife. Without saying a word, she motioned to the hanger that was in her right hand and smiled. He slowly closed his eyes, inhaled deeply, and grabbed the hanger. Martha leaned in and kissed him gently on the cheek and then patted him on the back. "Now, go get that son of a bitch," she said. Dante picked up his phone began typing a reply to Scott, "Meet me at my house. We're going to New York City."

Laying the hanger down on their bed, Dante reached down, grasped the zipper on the bag with his right hand, and pulled down, opening the bag wide. Martha looked on in anticipation as he grabbed the suit that she had made for him to wear to do what heroes do. Lifting it up, Dante observed the mostly black suit, which was adorned with a wide vertical yellow stripe running from his left shoulder down to his waist. He put the suit on and took a couple of steps in it while Martha looked on adoringly. "That's my man," she said as she hugged him.

Before he left the house, he bent down and picked Bethany up from the swing. He held her above his head and brought her back down, placing her gently on his chest. He rocked back and forth and rubbed his hand over her head. Hesitantly, he handed her over to his wife, kissed her on the forehead, and walked to the door. As he pulled the door open, he was startled by Scott, who was wearing a similar outfit but with green instead of yellow. Scott's suit was equipped with rockets in his boots and gloves that allowed him to fly and maintain flight over a long period of time and distance. Before walking out the door, Dante paused to look back at his family one more time. "Go ahead, baby. We'll be here when you get back. New York needs you...the world needs you," Martha said as she blew him a kiss.

With that, Dante stepped out of the house and stood side by side with Scott. "Let's go," he said, and the two stepped to the edge of the porch, leapt into the air, and flew over the city, making their way across the country to face an enemy who was striking again. However, this time the enemy was striking with more force and ferocity than ever before. Knowing all this, the two flew through the air toward a foe that would not hold back, and they swore that they would not hold back either. The war was just beginning.

Chapter Fifteen

Amid the swirling snow, blaring sirens, flashing lights, and desperate pleas for help stood the calming presence of the purveyor of the magnificent level of violence and destruction that had descended onto West 34th Street. Chaos reigned as mangled cars, trucks, and buses were strewn about, telephone poles were uprooted and leaning against the surrounding buildings; no one was safe.

Seventy-Two stood at the center of a large circular area that seemed unphased by the devastation and elements around him. He casually paced through the carnage, his circumference of calm around him, biding his time, almost as if he knew someone was coming to oppose him.

He continued to take inventory of the destruction he brought upon the city then he peered over to his right and noticed a small group of civilians herding together near a store front that had long since locked its doors. One of the men in the group stood up, brandished a pistol, and aimed it in the direction of the villainous Special before him. "Poor fool," Seventy-Two muttered as he outstretched his arm, opened his hand, and in one swift motion, closed it. In an instant, the man crumpled into a sickening heap at the feet of the others in the group. As the grin on his face grew wider, Seventy-Two swung his arm quickly to the right and the group of approximately a dozen civilians were sent barreling through the air towards a fixture of burning cars that his cohorts had set up to keep others at bay.

In a strange way, he looked at the destruction he had caused and felt at ease being at the center of it. He was overcome by a feeling of accomplishment and resounding peace. He thought about how this was all part of his mission. The government made decisions and took actions that should have been viewed as reprehensible, yet he was immediately viewed as the villain. From that moment, he'd vowed to give the world a reason to see him in that light. *I'll bring them to their knees. It is my only option.*

He lowered himself back to street level and was met by three police cruisers forming a barricade approximately twenty yards ahead of him. Those three police cruisers stood between him and six heavily armored and armed officers, all of whom had their weapons pointed at him.

"You just won't learn, will you? Can you not see that you are not in control here? You hide behind your guns, just as you always have. But I... I alone am the one in control. Look around you. Hundreds have died today because of your irresponsibility, your lack of willingness to recognize that I represent a revolution. This is only the beginning. New York City will fall... and I will rise," he said as he raised both hands in front of him and caused the police cruisers to launch high into the air.

The officers who were behind the vehicles stood up together, shoulder to shoulder. Each seemed to be unmoved by the show of force that was on display in front of them. Each officer pulled their face shield down on their riot helmets and together, walked in unison toward their target.

As they were moving forward through the snow blanketed street, four of the officers stopped and knelt down, holding their aim on Seventy-Two. The other two officers took several more steps before stopping just short of their target. The lead officer raised his gun and aimed at Seventy-Two's forehead.

"Control this," the man said defiantly as he pulled the trigger and sent the bullet spiraling through the winter air.

Appearing annoyed by this attempt at taking his life, Seventy-Two reached out ahead of him and pinched his index finger down to his thumb, quickly halting the momentum of the deadly projectile between his fingers. "Is this what you want?" he asked as he slammed the bullet against his forehead repeatedly before launching it through two civilians who were fleeing the area. Seventy-Two jumped into the air and flipped over the officers who were blocking his path. In one movement, he grabbed the pistol from one of the four officers who were holding the back of the line and shot an energy blast toward the ground which vaulted them into the air and sent them crashing into a snow drift on the side of the road.

"This will do nothing. NOTHING!" he shouted as he placed the barrel of the gun to his temple and pulled the trigger five times. Each bullet that exited the chamber slammed into his head and fell to the ground, causing no damage. Out of frustration, he bent the weapon in half and allowed it to fall harmlessly to his feet. "See, nothing." He shrugged, turning away from the officers.

"New York will never fall!" shouted someone from a distance. Sighing calmly, Seventy-Two turned around and gazed up at the Empire State Building, which towered above them and cast an intimidating shadow below.

"Is that right?" he asked as he began to hover above the street. He lowered his head and began to inhale and exhale deeply. As his breaths increased in speed, he raised his arms and brought his hands together just in front of his chest. Suddenly, his eyes began to glow red and a stream of energy emerged from the corners of both eyes.

His hands began to glow a fiery red and yellow; he extended both arms with his palms outward and pointed them in the direction of the Empire State Building. "Fall," he said, firing a massive energy beam through the twelfth floor of the building. "Fall," he said again as he sent another shot through the building, this time ten floors higher than the first. "Fall," he repeated as he moved to send another blast through the building. But just as he thrust his hands outward, the glowing stopped and he began to plummet toward the ground below him.

Disoriented, he tried to regain his composure. He was shaken by what just happened. He had yet to feel a moment of weakness and was taken aback by this event. "No, this can't be happening. Not yet," he said as he pulled himself back to his feet.

His hands were shaking and his legs were unstable beneath him. He wondered if anyone had seen him fall to the ground and fail to sustain his attack on the building. Stubbornly, he forced himself to stand upright even with his legs trembling beneath him. Internally, he acknowledged this moment and what it meant: even he had limits, and he just reached them. Now was not the time to push himself any further. Now was the time to gather himself and allow himself time to leave before suffering any additional setbacks.

He launched himself into the air, but was quickly met with a rapidly flying Dante who aimed himself at the villain's stomach. The two continued together in the air and began to fall back to the ground. As they were falling, Dante took several shots at Seventy-Two's face. With each punch that landed, Seventy-Two's mask shifted slightly and began to show signs of damage He landed the punches and, on the final blow, Dante was able to see blood beginning to drip from the bottom of his adversary's mask. The Special who had been bulletproof just moments before was now being injured by simple fisticuffs.

Gathering as much energy as he could, Seventy-Two shot an energy blast from his hands to Dante's chest, sending the hero flying backwards into Scott's arms. He descended to the ground and placed Dante down beside him. Scott stepped forward and made eye contact with Seventy-Two, who was just bringing himself to a standing position. The two maintained eye contact, but did not move any further. Seventy-Two tilted his head to the side as Scott squinted as if he was losing sight of who was before him through the falling snow. Seventy-Two ran his hand along the blood on his chin and stared at it intently before being gathered by his two partners and taken off into the sky.

"What the hell was that all about?!?" shouted Dante as he began walking toward Scott. "Do you hear me?!? What was that?" he continued. Scott did not take his eyes off of the spot he'd last seen Seventy-Two standing. He just continued staring.

"Scott! People died here and you just let him go? Explain yourself!" Dante screamed louder, pushing his friend from behind causing Scott to fall to the ground. "I can't," he said, bringing himself back to his feet. "I can't."

Chapter Sixteen

"Terry Monahan, reporting for Satellite News Network. Rescue crews comprised of paramedics, police officers, and volunteers have spent much of the night digging through the rubble and debris that has fallen from the Empire State Building, searching desperately for survivors. The initial death toll has climbed upwards of five-hundred, and the fear shared amongst the first responders on the scene is that the number will double before the sun rises in the morning," the veteran reporter said solemnly as she stood amongst the smoking piles of rubble and burnt vehicles strewn about behind her.

Images of smoke billowing from the iconic New York City landmark brought back memories of the terrorist attacks that shook the nation to its core and ultimately brought the population closer together, if only for a short while. The resolve of the city had been tested again, having just faced an unprecedented attack from an enemy unlike any that had been encountered in the past.

The reporter continued to traverse through the wreckage while grasping onto the arm of a member of the armed forces. Her unrivaled composure, a longstanding staple of her reporting through the years, was on full display as she navigated through the scene to perform a task that she had repeatedly done effortlessly during her career. It was as if she could simply flip a switch and remove herself from the emotions that would overcome most and report the destruction, devastation, and damage to a nation that needed to know. To a nation that needed her more than they wished to acknowledge.

Meanwhile, on the opposite side of the country, Dante and Scott landed quietly in Dante's backyard. The two remained separated once they touched down, standing there silently, as they had been during the long trek back home from the East Coast.

Dante, who was pacing back and forth beneath the starlit sky, exuded frustration. He raised his hands to his face as he attempted to wipe away the anger that he was harboring for his longtime friend. Stopping abruptly, he spun around and charged toward Scott, reached his arms out, gripped the collar of his uniform then raised him up above him.

"What was that, Scott?!? What in the hell were you thinking? You had him and…and you just froze," Dante said with his lips quivering as he was overcome with emotion. "So many people died. At his hands, nonetheless. And you froze. You froze…" Dante's voice trailed off as he lowered Scott back to the ground.

Scott remained silent in the well-manicured backyard and brushed himself off while he tried to compose himself enough to craft a response. Not just any response, but one that would do justice to the epic failure that he felt he was now.

"I'm no hero," Scott began. "I'm not like you. I can't leap into burning buildings and take entire families to safety from what seemed like an inescapable death. I'm not built like that. Shit, I mean, my most well-known ability is that

I can disappear. I'm good at hiding, Dante!" Scott said. Tears welled up in his eyes as he began to grasp the full extent of what had happened in New York City. Images of innocent civilians lying in the street and trapped in their cars, dying, ran through his mind.

"I have never been able to do what you do," he continued. "Without hesitation, you step into danger and it's almost like you don't consider what is at risk when you put yourself in the situations that you do," Scott said as his frustrations began to mount.

Taken aback, Dante sat down on an iron bench beneath an oak tree which towered over the pair. "Yeah, I get it. You don't think you can do what I do. Sure, it seems like I'm invincible. Bullets ricochet off me, right?" Dante said, leaning back and resting his arms atop the bench. "Scott, I have put myself in the situations that you described because I can. Not because I want to...but because I have to. I have these abilities for a reason. I have been given these powers to do some good in this world. Even if this world hates me, I must love this world. And I do that by showing the world what love is. I do that by defending this world, even when it attacks me and tries to take me to the ground."

"And that's where we differ!" Scott shouted. "This world hates us. Sure, there's a small pocket of people who give a damn, understand what we are, but the majority of people see us as what's wrong with the world. We are freaks to them. And you know damn well how they treat people who are different, right? They cast them out and leave them for dead. Why would that ever change? And yes, that is something that I have a hard time looking past," he said as he stomped the ground beneath him.

"You want to know why I didn't go after Seventy-Two?" Scott continued. "You're not the only one, Dante. I do too. I froze because there was a moment that I felt a sense of familiarity. I felt like I was at peace for a brief moment. Even with all of the chaos around us and that bothers me. It bothers me that I can't be a hero like you. No matter how hard I try. I can't do it."

Dante stood up from the bench and walked toward his friend, who had sunk to the ground and cupped his face in his hands. Dante placed his arms under Scott's and helped raise him to his feet. Looking into his eyes, Dante wiped the tears away from Scott's face and stared at him for a moment.

"We don't stop here. This doesn't define us. And yes, I said 'us' intentionally. We are in this together. Scott and Dante against the world, right? Do you remember what you said when we first got our suits?" Dante asked.

"Let's change the world," Scott replied.

"You're damned right! Let's change the world. Let's bring it together, even while it seems like it's okay with being torn apart. Let's do the right thing in the face of those who would do the opposite. Because quite frankly, Scott, I need you by my side while we do this. I can't do it alone and I wouldn't have wanted anyone else beside me other than you. Let's change the world," Dante said as he wrapped his arms around his friend and hugged him tightly.

As the two separated following their embrace, Scott shook his arms and straightened his posture at the same time as he placed his hands onto Dante's shoulders. "You're right, Dante," he said. "I know that we've been gifted these abilities because we can handle them and use them for what they were intended to be used for. I can guarantee you that next time, I will not freeze when I am in the position to act. When it's my time to make a move, I will strike without hesitating." Scott's mood was markedly different from what it had been just moments before.

The tension in the air could be felt for blocks. Scott went from being weak and disappointed in himself to feeling invincible in seconds. Dante had that effect on people and put that particular skillset to use whenever he needed to motivate those around him. The two stood there in silence for a moment as the sound of crickets and cicadas began to increase in volume around them.

Chapter Seventeen

The most challenging aspect of changing the world presented itself in the form of hidden adversaries. After the attack on New York City and the devastation of the Empire State Building, Seventy-Two went radio silent and eventually off the radar altogether. The lulls between catastrophic events allowed Dante to focus on his philanthropic efforts in the city in which he was born.

Martha's energy shined brightly when the couple, along with Scott and Steve put on events like neighborhood block parties and Thanksgiving feasts for the homeless. She jumped to the forefront during these events and felt that even though she did not have powers like her husband and his friends, she was able to impact others in a way that she could not have imagined before. She was making a difference. She was special, too.

Dante, Scott, and Steve worked diligently to fight criminal activity near and far and had been dubbed the "Special Forces" by the media. The name, while initially scoffed at by Scott, was accepted by the trio and they welcomed it as they continued to advance their cause of justice and peace.

Unfortunately, bringing change to a world that usually fears the mere thought of change as well as those who are different from most presented more threats than they had been prepared for. Sure, they understood that they would be getting into confrontations that would, more often than not, be physical. But they could not have imagined the type of terror that would come to their very doorstep.

On a rainy Los Angeles night in November, a black 2000 model Buick Century sat alone in an alleyway in the industrial district. Rain pelted the vehicle and lightning streaked across the darkened sky, illuminating the clouds and skyline below. In the dimly lit alley, the Buick ominously sat idly with its driver side door opened and hazard lights blinking. Aside from the rain and thunder, the only sound to be heard in this area was the sound of the windshield wiper blades streaking across the windshield. As the wiper blades moved left to right, clearing off the falling rain, blood spatter was exposed on the interior side of the windshield as well as the outline of a body slumped over the driver's side seat onto the center console.

Soon, the sound of sirens filled the air as an EMT vehicle and police cruiser raced to the scene through the monsoon that was growing increasingly more intense and impactful by the moment. The alleyway that had been obstructed by a pair of vehicles and another pair of officers setting up a perimeter around the area. One plain-clothed gentleman, Detective Bryson Alexander, stood off to the side of the throughway with the woman who had discovered the scene and immediately reported it to the authorities. Alexander concluded his conversation with the witness, who leaned against the building. He lit the cigarette that was resting between his lips and began to walk in the direction of the Buick that rested alone in the alley.

Reaching into his jacket pocket, Alexander grabbed a pair of latex gloves and pulled them on. He reached into the vehicle and turned the key in the ignition to shut the car down. Raising his flashlight, he shone the light onto the body. The beam revealed a gruesome sight which immediately gave credibility to the witness's shocked and traumatized demeanor. The body was riddled with gunshot wounds through the torso, and, inexplicably, the individual's head had been ripped from its body, but was nowhere to be found.

Detective Alexander began to rummage through the victim's pockets, looking for a formal piece of identification. The license plate had been removed from the vehicle and the VIN was scratched off the tags inside - not that that meant anything, around here. This could be another drug deal gone wrong with the victim being a criminal who stole the vehicle and got caught up with the wrong cartel. Bryson had seen this scenario play out often in his young career, but his intuition was pointing him in another direction.

Unable to collect anything of value from the victim's pockets, he grabbed the man's wrists and was shocked to find that the fingertips had been cut off and were nowhere in the vicinity of the scene. The detective stepped back from the vehicle and bent down, placing his hands on his knees as he tried to gather his thoughts.

The ferocity of the storm had subsided slightly as the investigation continued under the dark blanket of clouds above. Los Angeles has had its fair share of gruesome brutality over the years and hell, Detective Alexander had found himself in the middle of many of the recent occurrences. But this one was different. This was too precise. Too personal.

Alexander worked his way around the vehicle, shining his flashlight on the ground and across the Buick as he walked slowly and methodically through the rain. Inhaling deeply for a moment, he reached his hand to his mouth and grabbed the cigarette butt from it and flicked it into the air. Just as the remnants of the cigarette began to flip through the air, it was snatched before it hit the ground. Dante stood before the detective with a smirk on his face. "Littering, Detective? I pegged you for a better man than that," he said jokingly.

Shaking his head, Alexander put his hands up slowly. "You got me, hero."

"What do we have here?" Dante asked as placed the cigarette butt between his thumb and index finger, flicking it into a dumpster at the end of the alley.

"Well, I have a homicide victim. Not the of the average variety, either. Multiple gunshot wounds, fingertips removed, and head… missing. Gone," Detective Alexander replied.

"Any witnesses?" Dante pressed on.

"Just the woman who came across the vehicle while she was walking by. No forms of identification either. Plates and VIN are gone," Alexander continued.

With a puzzled look on his face, Dante peered into the vehicle. He was able to tell that the victim was male, but that was about it.

Dante lifted himself into the air and began to look around the scene from above. With the rain beginning to fall more heavily, he lowered himself back to street level and reached into the car. "Hey! Gloves!" Alexander shouted. Rolling his eyes, Dante reached back towards the detective, put the gloves on, then continued his search.

"I know... I know... I know..."

"I get it, Dante. You know," said Alexander.

"That wasn't me," Dante replied solemnly. The voice reverberated through Dante's bones as it continued to repeat. Focusing, Dante was able to zero in on where the voice was emanating from; it was a recording device that was affixed to the underside of the driver's seat. He removed it and stepped back from the car.

The fluctuation in the storm began to rise again, and the rain fell at a rate that caused gutters to overflow and spill out onto the streets beneath them. With the rain pouring down over his face, Dante gathered his composure and pressed the rewind button on the device. He looked at

Detective Alexander stoically. The detective lowered his flashlight and walked over to Dante, who was now using the wall of the warehouse beside the Buick to hold himself up. Bryson placed his hand on Dante's shoulder and with that signal of assurance, Dante pressed "Play."

"Why are you doing this?" a shaking voice asked.

"Oh, you know why. Don't play dumb. I cannot stand idly by while the world looks at what was done to people like us without acting. I would be as guilty as they are," a different, distorted voice replied. "You know who I am, don't you?" that same voice asked before gunshots could be heard on the recording.

"I know... I know... I know" murmured the victim in response just as the recording came to a stop. In that very instant, an object fell from above and landed on the hood of the car before rolling off and at the feet of Dante and Detective Alexander.

The Detective pointed his flashlight at the ground and the light revealed the severed head of the victim. Dante immediately recognized who the man was now, and it nearly broke him. It was Steve, and it pained him deeply that his friend's life ended in such a horrific way. He struggled to contain his emotions, but tears began flowing freely as he was overcome with grief. He clenched his fists, and screamed at the sky, then looked down at what was left of his friend.

Detective Alexander bent down and grabbed a sheet of paper that was attached to a rope wrapped around Steve's head, through his open mouth. Standing back up, the detective opened the folded sheet and read the words aloud: "Let's change the world."

Chapter Eighteen

The ripple effect of Steve's murder was felt by millions. Dante, Martha, Scott, and Steve had been spending countless hours to bridge the divide between typical humans and the Specials who had been thrust into the spotlight since Seventy-Two and Dante burst onto front pages and social media sites around the globe. The quartet of friends spent any free time they had on good will efforts which were met overwhelmingly with positivity, which made Steve's murder even more shocking and hard to come to terms with.

"Let's change the world." Four words that haunted Dante since he read the paper that was affixed to Steve's severed head. Those very words had been shared by Dante to crowds, interviewers, and allies alike over the past few years and that made it increasingly more difficult to determine who was responsible for the murder. Dante wrestled with what felt like insurmountable grief but tried to keep his pain under control when he was around Scott, Martha, and especially his young daughter, Bethany.

The day of the funeral service was a solemn one. The rain that fell the night that Steve had been murdered had not stopped falling and Dante refused to believe that the two events were not related. Dark gray clouds spanned across the sky as the rain continued from above, and the occasional rumble of thunder could be heard. News vans lined the road directly outside the cemetery where the service was being held and just outside the iron fence that encircled the cemetery was an army of police officers who stood between the service and the reporters who were hoping to catch a glimpse of who was attending the funeral, or to get a quote from one of the individuals who were grieving on the other side.

Little Bethany was adorned in a black dress that seemed meant for someone much older than her and holding a pink Hello Kitty umbrella. Dante stood holding her, alongside Martha who wrapped her arms around Dante's right arm while she rested her head on his shoulder. Scott stood nearby; his hands clasped in front of him.

The rain streamed down Scott's face as the pastor delivered his message and final prayer before ending the service and allowing family and friends to pay their respects prior to the casket being lowered into the ground. Scott had taken Steve's death particularly hard. Not that anyone took it lightly, but Scott had shut down in the days that followed the news of his friend's murder. In fact, this was the only day that he had exited his home since Dante made the fateful phone call to let him know what happened. Their friend was gone, and there were no leads to indicate who had committed the crime. Not one.

As the pastor stepped away from the podium, which stood to the left of the casket, he signaled for those who were in attendance to step forward. Scott stood up and walked away from the area, which resulted in a rapid flow of flashes from cameras and smartphones just outside the cemetery. Taking notice of this, Dante moved Bethany to one hip and reached his hand out to hold Martha's. The three made their way to the casket, stopping first to look at a large photograph of Dante, Scott, and Steve that had been taken at one of their recent fundraising events in Los Angeles.

Once they reached the burial site, Martha released her grasp of Dante's hand and placed her right hand gently onto the casket for a moment before stepping to the side to allow Dante to have an extra moment. Closing his eyes and lowering his head, memories flooded Dante's mind, and he eventually allowed a smile to creep onto his face.

Taking notice of the smile, Bethany wrapped her arms around her Daddy's neck and gently kissed his cheek. "Uncle Stevie, huh Daddy?" Bethany whispered softly.

"Yeah, baby. Uncle Stevie." Dante replied as one tear fell from his eye and traversed down the same cheek that was just kissed by his daughter.

Standing there, Dante remembered the first time he'd met Steve in high school. Steve was trying to recruit some of the students to work at the diner, and Dante was one of the first who took him up on the offer. Dante always said that Steve was a hell of a salesperson, and that his pitch was the reason he agreed to work there. Steve always argued that it was the free meal during shifts and the milkshakes. Yeah, had to be the milkshakes.

Under the slowly clearing skies, Dante and Bethany laid two roses on top of the casket. After another moment of silence, Dante kissed his hand and held it out for Bethany, who kissed it just before he placed his hand on top of the casket that held his friend. "We love you, Steve. I'll find who did this and make them face the consequences of their actions," Dante quietly promised. Turning away from the grave site, Dante noticed that Scott was standing just outside the gate and was surrounded by reporters.

"Yeah, I'm pissed!" Scott yelled in response to a question presented by one of the local media members. "We've done nothing but try to help. Dante has been busting his ass out here trying to help you! We've been doing everything we can to make you see that we're not monsters and this is how we're repaid. Is this the gratitude that you mean to show us? And not just that, but Steve is dead!

Murdered by someone who has yet to be identified and all you can do is try to advance your careers by standing outside a cemetery while family and friends grieve the loss of a loved one. What if it was your friend? What if he was your brother? How dare you stop me to ask questions about my fallen friend!" Scott screamed while Dante handed Bethany over to Martha and made a beeline to his side.

Many of the media members in attendance had lowered their cameras and cellphones at this point, but Scott was not done yet. "So, you want a headline, huh? Well, here's a headline for you assholes!" Scott said, raising his hands, causing the devices to be ripped from the hands of those who held them. In a show of power and anger, Scott allowed the items to float in the air for a moment. Dante walked alongside his friend, and Scott took notice, briefly locking eyes with him before he slammed the devices to the ground, shattering the equipment.

"There's your headline," Scott said, storming away from the cemetery. In this moment, Dante found himself in a rare instance of being unable to find words for those around

him. Since he had taken the very public stance of a hero,

Dante had grown increasingly comfortable as the mouthpiece

for those who could not speak for themselves and a calming

presence in the face of adversity.

One of the reporters reached into his jacket pocket,

grabbed a small spiral bound notepad and pencil. The reporter

raised his hand and looked directly into Dante's eyes, awaiting

the moment in which Dante would choose him and approve

his request to speak.

Rolling his eyes, Dante nodded his head in the

direction of the reporter. "Uh, yeah. Hi, Mr. Dante… Marcus

Watson from Channel 6 News at Noon. Just wanted to get

your thoughts on what just happened," the reporter said

nervously.

Inhaling deeply, Dante checked around himself to

make sure his wife and daughter were not nearby. "Well,

Marcus Watson. My thoughts are dark. We are burying my

friend, a member of my family, at this very moment. I'm

shaken. Not broken, but shaken. I'm saddened as well. But not just because one of my closest friends is dead, but because of people like you. You all stand here hoping for a quote or something notable to print or report on television," Dante said while walking back and forth, trying to remain composed.

"Scott is hurt, too. And I'm sure not a single person on this side of the fence tried to express sympathy for his plight. No, instead you bombarded him with questions as he was exiting a painful place. You managed to magnify that pain, amplify it to a point that he acted in a way in which he typically wouldn't have. Now, please don't get it twisted. I love you all. Regardless of your actions, I love you all. But this seems a bit much, don't you think?" Dante asked as Martha and Bethany reached his side.

The sunshine had made its way through the clearing clouds above as Dante continued to speak to the reporters. Realizing the reporters' equipment was in tatters on the ground, Dante pulled out his cellphone and handed it to his wife. Dante picked Bethany up and signaled for Martha to hit record on the phone. "Just in case you are wondering, the mission remains the same. I am unwilling to allow any one act against us to derail us from accomplishing what we set out to in the beginning. As I said, I love you all and I will stand with you in your darkest times. I just ask that you stand by us in ours."

While he was speaking to the camera and the reporters in front of him, Dante noticed that Bethany was watching him with a wide smile on her face. "Hey baby, what do you want to do?" he asked. With a confidence that was well beyond her years, Bethany looked over at her mom and right back at Dante. "Change the world, Daddy. Let's change the world."

Chapter Nineteen

Sitting on the last stool of the bar counter at Jimmy's Pub, Scott stared downward at his nearly empty glass of whiskey. Clad in a much different outfit than he had worn at Steve's funeral, Scott wore a black zip-up hooded jacket, camo hat, and jeans in order to keep his identity hidden from the others in the bar. Where Dante seemed to relish in the spotlight that came with public heroism, Scott tended to be more reserved when it came to his private life. He did not want that line to become blurred.

Jimmy's was a popular hangout and was particularly busy this evening. But even with all of the people buzzing all around him, Scott seemed to be unphased by the volume of the music and rowdiness of the crowd. Reaching his hand out, he gently grabbed his glass and swirled it around before taking a swig and finishing the rest of his drink.

Scott's attention was taken from his empty glass and the bartender, who'd apparently forgotten he was sitting at the bar, and redirected his focus to the television which was replaying the footage that was recorded from the funeral earlier in the day. Scott caught a glimpse of himself on the screens above the bar and he saw a look in his eyes that took him by surprise. Knowing that he had been overcome with grief in that moment, he could see a look of unmitigated rage in his eyes. The moment just before he destroyed the reporter's equipment, they held a red glare that he had never seen before. This should have startled him, but he found himself liking it, embracing it.

"Hey, shut that shit off!" yelled a man leaning against the wall next to the jukebox. "No one wants to see those freaks!" he continued as he slammed his bottle of Miller Lite to the ground.

Embarrassed, the woman who was accompanying him hurried to the ground to clean up the shards of glass that had spread across the floor. Since no one moved to change the channel or turn the televisions off, the man sloppily moved himself away from the wall and staggered forward one slow and shaky step before noticing that his female companion was beneath him, cleaning up after him. With his right hand, he reached down and clenched a fistful of her platinum blonde hair in his hand and yanked her up from the ground, forcing her to one of the stools behind them.

"Strike one," Scott murmured.

The man continued to shove his way through the crowd toward the bar. "I said, turn the fucking TV off, asshole," the man demanded as he leaned up against the bar. The bartender, apparently accustomed to this type of aggression, continued on with her business. "You deaf or something?" the man shouted before he swung his outstretched arms in front of him, causing the drinks that were sitting atop the bar to fly into the air.

"Strike two," Scott whispered.

The woman made her way from the stool through the crowd, trying to catch up with her significant other, who may have had one too many to drink. "Daryl, I think you need to calm down," she pleaded with him, placing her hand on his back and rubbing gently in a circular motion. For a moment, it looked as if he actually considered doing as she said, but that moment passed quickly as he swung his left arm backward and his hand made contact with her face, sending her crumbling to the ground.

"Strike three," Scott spoke aloud, pushing back from the bar and walking toward the pair. Daryl, red-faced and reeling slightly, raised his right hand and stared down at the woman who was trying to calm him, holding her hand out to protect herself.

The crowd quickly dispersed as Scott walked slowly and methodically forward. The woman looked up at Daryl, tears streaming down her cheeks, the same cheeks that had played host to similar tears in the past, and cowered in fear of what was to come next.

Time slowed down to a crawl as Scott envisioned past beatings, very similar to the public display that was unfolding in front of him and the rest of the patrons in the bar. The same scene, but with different backdrops. The same tears, the same pain, the same reconciliation. A vicious cycle that would eventually come to a sad ending. *What would Dante do?* Scott

pondered. *Talk. Dante would talk, but he wouldn't really do*

anything. His words would do nothing...not really. He would

talk them down, the two would go home, and he would beat

her again. Possibly to death. But, hey...he would have made his

point, right?

"Not tonight. Not me," Scott said to himself as he

closed in on the two.

The bartender reached behind her and grasped the

phone that was sitting atop its charger and began to dial 911.

Scott flicked his wrist and caused the electricity to short out in

the bar, and suddenly the phone went dead. "Shit!" she

shouted, feeling additionally pissed off because she'd left her

cell phone inside her purse in the trunk of her car.

"I've told you to not put your hands on me like that,

woman!" Daryl shouted. For a moment, it appeared as if he

was going to strike her again, but he lowered his hand briefly

before reaching it back up to the counter and grabbing a

bottle of beer that was left unattended. He looked down at

her and smiled. It was a smile that she had seen many times over the years. It looked as if Daryl was coming to his senses. She slowly stood back up in front of him and looked deeply into his eyes.

This is it. Scott thought. He felt that this was the moment that the two would reconcile and exit Jimmy's together. He found himself hoping that the couple would leave behind any traces of domestic abuse or drunken stupidity as they left together. That image was quickly shattered as Daryl slammed the bottle against the bar counter, wrapped his left arm around his girlfriend, and spun her, forcing her back against his chest and raising the broken bottle to the left side of her neck.

With the glass pressed against her neck, Daryl looked at the bartender who stood, aghast. "All you had to do was turn off the damned TV. Now, her blood is on your hands," he said as he increased pressure, causing blood to slowly trickle down his love's neck and onto her black and pink blouse.

"How about if I turn the TV off?" asked Scott. "Will you let her go?" he asked with his arms spread out to his sides.

Squinting his eyes, Daryl tried to focus in on the face of the man who stood before him. Even with the attempts at concealing his identity from those around him, Scott could tell that Daryl had identified him. Maybe it was his voice that gave it away or perhaps it was the red gleam in his eyes. Scott had the sensation that the strange attribute had revealed itself again; he felt a faint heat and his vision sharpened, the same way it had when the reporters were pressing him at the funeral.

Realizing he was in too deep to alter his course, Daryl shook his head, attempting to dismiss any fear or trepidation that was floating around in his heavily intoxicated mind. Unwavering, Daryl increased the pressure of the broken bottle on his girlfriend's neck, causing more blood to trickle from the wound. Scott raised his hand and pointed his right index finger at the televisions above the bar and he flicked the finger against his thumb, causing the televisions to come back on, each one now featuring a sporting event.

"Don't you take one more step, you… you monster!" Daryl shouted, appearing increasingly nervous.

"I'm not the monster here. I think you know that. You're scared now and I completely understand that," Scott said calmly. "You should be. You messed up and think there is no way that you can get out of here without causing more harm. But you can. I want you to consider your next move very closely, for it can greatly alter the outcome of this situation," Scott concluded, looking directly into Daryl's eyes.

"Oh, I have considered my next move very closely you FREAK!" Daryl shouted, pointing the broken bottle at Scott then thrusting it forcefully back to the tender place it had just been cutting. Scott knew that in this moment he had to decide on one of two actions. Number one was to use his abilities to redirect Daryl's hand, causing the bottle to harm no one. The other choice, ultimately the one he chose, was to neutralize Daryl.

As Daryl's broken bottle wielding hand came down toward his girlfriend's neck, Scott shot an energy blast directly through the left side of Daryl's neck, gushing streams of blood out onto the floor below. The woman ran from his arms and fell to the ground just feet away. "You bastard!" she yelled toward Scott. "He wasn't going to hurt me! *What have you done?!*".

"He already has hurt you. He's ruined you, you just fail to see it." Scott said solemnly. Inside, he felt that he'd made the right decision. If he found himself in this exact scenario, Dante may have chosen to disarm Daryl; that would not have stopped him from arriving at his final destination. Daryl would have killed her. It would not have been pleasant. He would have made her suffer and she would have been the first in a potential long line of victims. Scott took solace in the understanding that he'd stopped Daryl from hurting her or anyone else again.

Standing over Daryl as he slowly perished at his feet, Scott thought to himself: *This had to happen. You did the right thing.* Wiping both eyes with his hands, Scott turned around and observed the crowd that remained. Some were ducked beneath tables, and others stood defiantly, holding their cellphones and recording his every move. After taking a moment to look around the room, he stepped towards the bar.

The bartender, who had hidden behind the counter, peered out at Scott over the top of the empty bar. Pulling up the zipper of his jacket, Scott reached into his jeans pocket to grab a fifty-dollar bill. He glared down at Daryl as his girlfriend wrapped her arms around his lifeless body.

"Keep the change," Scott said as he placed the bill on the bar counter.

Chapter Twenty

In the beginning, it was simple. Sweet conversations and longing stares from two star-crossed lovers in the making. Dante, a mysterious young man who had all of the attributes and personality of the star quarterback of any high school or college football team but without the ego that accompanied most of them. Martha, the quiet yet immensely popular daughter of the town's pastor, with charm and a smile that could brighten the darkest of nights. The relationship that bloomed from such humble beginnings was similar to those written about by authors like Capote and Shakespeare.

Their fateful first night out which had opened her and the world's, eyes to the Specials who had begun to emerge should have been a red flag for Martha, and quite frankly, would have been a red flag for any other young woman. Except Martha was not like any other young woman, and Dante was clearly not like any other young man. Martha was drawn to Dante's integrity, strength, and positivity. From almost the very beginning, she could tell that she was falling for him and that he felt the same.

After Bethany was born, Dante had promised Martha that he would try to be around more. In the first years of their marriage, Dante found himself immersed in the hero lifestyle. Between battles with Seventy-Two and saving people from fires and other disasters, Dante's time spent at home with Martha had dwindled down drastically, leaving her to manage their non-profit community organization alone. Martha did not wilt in the face of the mounting tasks of their community efforts though. She faced these tasks head on because the message and purpose of the organization was one that she felt deep in her heart.

The most difficult part of Dante making that promise had been that they both knew that he would not be able to keep it. It's not like he would ever be able to turn a blind eye to the pain and suffering of the world. There always seemed to be something that popped up and required his intervention. A bank robbery, plane crash, or natural disaster would rip him from home and send him hurling into the sky towards another battle. The difficulty increased following Steve's murder. Dante became more withdrawn at home and spent more time patrolling the city. Martha knew that Dante blamed himself, even though she tried countless times to tell him that there was no way that he could be everywhere at once.

Standing in their bedroom, Martha wrapped her arms around Dante and tried to console him as he stood there, holding a picture of Martha, Scott, Steve and himself. "Please don't go. Stay with us," she whispered into his ear.

"I have to. The city needs me," Dante replied.

"We need you, Dante! I need you… your daughter needs you!" Martha said, raising her voice uncharacteristically.

Turning the photograph to face her, Dante wiped a tear from his cheek. "Steve needed me, too. And I wasn't there. He was killed and I didn't do anything about it."

"Because you *couldn't* do anything about it, Dante. There are terrible people in this world and they will do terrible things. People have robbed and killed others before you were here and will continue to do so long after you are gone. You cannot possibly think that you can stop every single one of them, can you? It's not fair to you or to us. I know that it's hard, baby. But, please remember that we are here with you. Don't leave us behind," Martha said.

Dante placed the photograph on their dresser and wrapped his arms around Martha, and, for a moment, it appeared as if he was going to consider her plea. He kissed her forehead gently and walked toward Bethany's bedroom. Pushing the door open softly, he peered in and saw his daughter clutching her pink teddy bear as she slept peacefully.

"There's my sunshine," he said, sitting down on the edge of her bed. Sitting there, memories rushed through his mind of the moment he got to hold her in the hospital room. Aside from the doctors, he was the first person to hold Bethany. Adorned in hospital scrubs, the doctor had handed his little girl over to him, and he was consumed with a happiness that he had never felt before. In that moment, he swore that he would love and protect her. Dante loved Martha with all his heart, but the feeling he got when he'd first held Bethany was unlike anything he had ever experienced.

Bethany's room was decorated with all things pink and unicorn. Pictures of Dante, Martha, and Bethany were hung on the wall next to the light switch, and a mountain of stuffed animals was piled in the corner of the room. This was his princess's safe place, and he was obsessed with keeping it that way. Dante found it hard to believe that his baby girl was already six years old. Time had flown faster than he cared to admit.

For a moment, he continued to rest on the edge of her bed, just watching her sleep. He brushed a stray strand of hair away from her face and tucked it gently behind her ear before he stood up. Carefully, he grabbed her blankets and pulled them up to her shoulders and tucked her in. He bent down and gently kissed her on the cheek. "You are my sunshine, Bethany. I love you," he said, turning and making his way to her door. He glanced back one last time and blew a kiss at his little girl, and he could have sworn he saw a smile creep up on the right side of her mouth.

"You're leaving, aren't you?" Martha asked. Dante nodded his head, unable to respond to her question vocally. "Please know that you cannot save everyone. That weight is too much for one man to carry on his shoulders. I love you, Dante. I want you to know that you don't owe anyone anything."

Looking at the calendar hanging on the wall, Dante noticed that January seventeenth was circled. The date represented one of the latest community efforts that the two had planned. "I'll be there. We will all be there. Me, you, Bethany, and Scott. We'll make it huge, too. DJs, food, celebrities, giveaways. You might be right about me not being able to save everyone, but we sure can help a lot of people," he said, smiling.

Martha flashed a grin that reminded Dante of the night she'd passed him her phone number in the diner. She looked truly happy again, if only for a moment. "Deal. Now get out of here, I have some planning to do," she said, causing them both to laugh in unison. She reached down and grabbed his hand and they walked to the back door. Without saying a word, the two looked into each other's eyes, kissed, and then Dante leapt into the air and flew off. With a tear falling down her cheek, she blew her husband a kiss.

Dante flew a short distance away to Jimmy's Pub, the site of the altercation between a drunk patron and an unidentified Special. When Dante had first heard of this, he had immediately felt uneasy. He knew that Scott was not in a good state of mind following his confrontation with the reporters covering Steve's funeral and he hoped that Scott had not crossed the line later that night.

Landing on the sidewalk in front of Jimmy's, Dante took note of a sign on the door that read "No Specials Permitted." Dante pushed the door open and stepped inside. The bar was significantly less crowded than it had been the night of the murder, but there were still several regulars sitting at booths in the back. No one was sitting at the bar, which left the bartender wiping the counter over and over again just to look busy.

Dante walked to the end of the bar and pulled the next to last stool out from beneath the counter. He sat patiently for a moment with his hands on the counter in front of him, waiting for the bartender to take notice of his presence. He looked around and tried to piece together the events that were reported. He saw the jukebox and then the televisions that had presumably sparked the violence. Those very same televisions were currently turned off, and Dante figured they had remained off since that night. The bartender made her way over and placed a drink menu down in front of him.

"What'll it be, big fella?" she asked, not really looking at him, which worked in his favor.

"Just a water…and a couple of answers." Dante responded.

"Oh God, not another reporter," the bartender responded, rolling her eyes. She grabbed a glass from behind the counter and filled it with ice and water before placing a small square napkin down and setting the glass on top of it in front of Dante.

"No, not a reporter. Just interested in finding out what happened that night," he responded just before taking a drink from the glass.

"What else is there to say?" she asked getting increasingly frustrated. "Daryl got drunk, hit his girl, threatened to cut her, actually cut her, and fucking paid for it. In my opinion, he got exactly what he deserved. That definitely wasn't the first time that asshole put his hands on a girl in this bar."

"Do you know who it was that stepped up to confront him? I know it was one of the Specials, but I need to know which one," Dante pressed on.

"He had a hat on and his hood up. I didn't really get a good look at his face, but…" Her voice trailed off as her gaze shifted to the booth in the back. "Earl said it looked like the guy that flipped out on the reporters earlier in the day. But no one got a clear look," she concluded before coming around and sitting on the stool next to Dante.

"Look, I know who you are. And to be honest, I hate the new sign that Jimmy put on the front door. But he wants us to be safe, ya know?" she said.

Dante nodded and thought: *Yeah, like there wasn't a broken bottle-wielding woman beater in the bar. The sign should say: No Drunk Redneck Douchebags Permitted.*

"Yeah, I get it," he said, taking another drink of his water.

"He sat right in that stool right next to where you're seated right now." The bartender continued. "Quiet as church mouse. Glass of whiskey and silence. That's all he wanted. Then Daryl had to go on and do Daryl shit."

"Thanks for your time. I really needed that water, and I appreciate your honesty. You have yourself a good night," Dante said, reaching into his wallet and grabbing the twenty-dollar bill from inside and placed it on the counter.

"Keep the change," the bartender said, shocking Dante and causing him to look back at her. "That's what he said to me before he left. 'Keep the change.'"

Dante nodded at her and exited the bar. *Keep the change...?* he thought, bewildered as he tried to piece everything together. "That son of a bitch. He knew I would come looking into this, and he left that message for me. What is happening with Scott? He's been off for a little while now, but this is starting to go too far."

Chapter Twenty-One

His phone sat on the kitchen counter, continuing to vibrate. Shaking his head in frustration, Scott stormed over to it, picked it up, and read the display. Seven missed calls from Dante and two unread text messages.

"We need to talk. Meet me in my backyard," read the latest text. Scott knew that Dante had found out that he had killed Daryl at Jimmy's and he was fine with that. Scott had tried telling Dante in the past that they were not alike. Sure, they were essentially raised together, but they came from different families. It was just a coincidence that they were both Specials. "I'm not like you, Dante! I'm not a hero!" The words he'd spoken to Dante in the very backyard he was being requested to visit rang through his head over and over. "I'm not a hero," he said to himself while he reached for the same hat and jacket that he'd worn that terrible night at Jimmy's.

A short time later, Scott hopped over the fence in Dante's backyard and as he landed on the other side, Dante stood up from the bench at the rear of the yard. "What are you doing on the seventeenth?" Dante asked.

Puzzled, Scott stared at Dante. This was not what he'd expected. He'd fully anticipated that Dante would come at him on his high horse and belittle him for what he had done. *Maybe he doesn't know what I did.* Scott thought. "Um, nothing. Why?" Scott asked.

"That's the day we're hosting the block party we have been planning for weeks. We have everything lined up and Martha, Bethany, and I want you to be there with us," Dante said.

"Count me in," Scott replied and with that, the two embraced each other for a moment before Dante grabbed Scott's shoulders and separated himself from his friend just enough to get a good look at what he was wearing.

"Is that the hat and jacket you wore to Jimmy's?" Dante asked.

"Yeah. It is," Scott replied. "Now, before you try to go lecturing me about how I should conduct myself as a member of the 'Special Forces', I want you to know that that bastard deserved exactly what he got!"

"Scott, that is not up to us!" Dante snapped back angrily. "We are not the judge, jury, and we are sure as hell not the executioner! I can't believe that I'm having this discussion with you. For as long as we've known each other, I never would have pegged you for a murderer."

Annoyed with the conversation they were having, Scott took a step back from Dante, looked up to the sky and then directly into Dante's eyes. "Yet here we are...you judging me. Dante, you fail to see that we are an endangered species. Or have you turned a blind eye to the fact that nearly as soon as Specials are being discovered, they go missing? Do you realize that Seventy-Two escaped from a government facility whose sole purpose was to perform experiments on these people who they capture?!?"

"Don't you dare try to make that sick bastard out to be some sort of sympathetic figure. He's no hero," Dante replied.

"And neither am I, Dante! I said that to you in this very yard, probably in this exact spot. I'm not like you. But, I'm not a bad guy, either. With Daryl, I acted with the best intentions at heart. He was going to kill that poor girl. And who knows if she would have been his first or last victim. For all we know, that sicko has killed women in the past and I just did the world a favor."

Dante stood in disbelief. Unable to come to grips with what his friend was saying to him. "Did the world a favor? By taking a life? Scott, you are better than that. You know that," he said as he began to process what Scott was really saying to him.

"Whoa, whoa, whoa... you said that with Daryl you acted with good intentions. Was there another time this happened?" Dante asked.

"That's bullshit, Dante. What do you mean?" Scott replied.

"I think you know what I mean. Where were you when Steve was killed? I feel sick even asking you this, but where the hell were you?" Dante shouted, pacing back and forth.

"You think I could kill Steve? You've lost your mind, man. I know his death hit us both hard, but I didn't think you could ever possibly look at me that way. He was my brother too. You've lost your grip on reality, man. I think you need some downtime. I'll handle the good-guy stuff while you take some time off," Scott replied.

"You... you'll handle the good-guy stuff? That's rich, Scott. Especially coming just days after you killed a man in a bar. But yeah, you can handle the good-guy stuff," Dante continued. In the awkward silence that followed, Dante saw that the light in the backyard was turned on by someone inside. This surprised him because Martha and Bethany had gone to sleep before he came outside to wait for Scott.

With his arms folded across his chest, Scott stood there, tapping his foot. "Do you have anything else you want to accuse me of, buddy? I think I want to go home now," he snapped at Dante.

"Okay, maybe I crossed the line about Steve. Of course I don't think you could do something like that. It's just, lately my emotions are getting the best of me. We've both had a hard few days. I'm sorry, man," Dante said.

"You 'maybe' crossed the line? You erased the line and danced all over the eraser shavings you dick. Yes, we've had a tough few days, but let me tell you, they will get better...and potentially worse. But we can't lose each other during the hard times. We're a team, man. That can't change."

"You're right. I'm sorry, Scott. Let's move past this. We have a block party to prep for," Dante said, extending his hand out towards Scott. For a moment, Scott looked down at Dante's hand and then back up at his eyes. Scott then reached out and shook his friend's hand and they embraced in a hug.

The back door creaked open and Bethany emerged from the shadows of the kitchen and into the shining light on the back-porch, wiping her eyes. "Daddy, why are you still up?" she asked.

Dante walked towards her and picked her up. "I'm just talking with Uncle Scott, sweetie.

"Yeah, baby girl. Me and your Daddy just had to figure some things out. I think we're good now though, right?" Scott asked, switching his focus to Dante.

"Yes. We're good now. Here, can you go to the furniture rental store tomorrow to pay for the tables and chairs we need for the seventeenth?" Dante asked, reaching into his pocket for a check he had written earlier in the night.

"Sure thing." Scott said taking the check from Dante.

"Great, thanks man. And hey, keep the change," Dante said before he walked back into his house and turned the backyard light off.

Chapter Twenty-Two

January 17, 2028 had arrived and with it came the block party that Martha, Dante, and Scott had been planning for months. Over the last few weeks, things had been relatively quiet for the team, and, as a result, Dante had been able to increase his attention, and, more effectively assist Martha with running their non-profit organization. Martha had been happy with this because she had recently felt part of the team instead of being alone, like she was for so long before Dante refocused his efforts on home.

The weather for the event was setting up to be perfect. Not a cloud in the sky, with temperatures in the mid-sixties. "This is perfect," Martha sang as she and Dante were sitting in the Communications Tent, sipping coffee together. Every minute they spent together recently was a highlight for her because of all the chaos that had preceded it. It had been weeks since Dante had to rush off and save someone else's day. Instead, he had been home, making his family's day. And she loved that more than anything.

Scott approached the tent holding Bethany, who was dressed in a flowing white dress with sunflowers printed all over it. "Alright, the DJs, tables, and food tents are all set up. Have you guys seen the line of people outside the gate?" Scott said smiling.

Martha and Dante stood up and peered out toward the crowd of people waiting to enter the block party.

"What do you say, Bethany? Want to start this party early?" Dante asked.

"Let's get this party started!" Bethany shouted.

The quartet known as the Special Forces made their way over to the gate and Dante grabbed a microphone from the DJ. "Ladies and gentlemen, thank you all for coming to this event today. It is our sincere hope that you all have a great time, network with some wonderful people, and eat some delicious food. I'm partial to my wife's thumbprint cookies. Please leave one for me!" Dante said as he signaled for the gate to be open.

As the crowd started to make their way into the party area, hundreds of people shook hands and hugged Dante, Martha, and Scott as they split up to visit the tents set up along the street. The party seemed to be off to a great start. Bethany ran off to be in the "Little Stars" area which was set up for with crafts, toys, and plenty of activities for the younger children. Martha and Dante were proud to see their daughter approaching all the other children and asking if they needed anything while they were playing before she took part in anything else.

"Train up a child in the way he should go; even when he is old, he will not depart from it. I think you guys are doing an outstanding job raising Bethany," Scott said proudly.

Dante reached his arm around his friend's shoulder and brought him in for a hug with Martha and him. The trio held onto each other for a moment longer and then Scott exited the tent and headed over to a group of men standing outside of a job placement tent.

"This place has it all, baby. How'd you pull it off?" Dante said while he and Martha walked around the party.

"Well, I had this handsome man helping me. It was nice to have a strong set of hands around to get this all organized. And you were there sometimes, too," Martha said erupting in laughter.

"Oh, is that right?" Dante asked, grabbing his wife and lifting her into the air with him, high above the party. "You did this, Martha. You brought joy to all these people. Look at all of them."

They looked down and observed everyone moving through the party. There were groups of people dancing near the DJ booths, eating meals together, and getting along peacefully. These were people of different races, religions, and backgrounds, yet here they were, existing together peacefully. No ulterior motives, just a peaceful festival. Dante and Martha hovered above the crowd for a few minutes more before Dante's eyes were drawn to an explosion several miles off in the distance. Martha's eyes widened and she locked eyes with her husband. Without saying a word, she approved of Dante leaving the party to help those that were near the blast.

Dante and Martha descended from the sky and landed near the Tiny Stars area. Bethany came rushing over and hugged them, nearly knocking them over. "Man, I love you guys," she said looking up at them.

"Hey baby, I have to leave for a little bit. I want you to stay with Mommy and Uncle Scott while I'm gone. You'll be safe here. I love you, sunshine," Dante said as he rubbed his nose against Bethany's and then gave her a kiss. Standing back up, Dante gave Martha a kiss then burst upward into the air and towards the direction of the blast.

"Where's he off to?" Scott asked.

"To save the day," Martha replied, a worried look in her eyes.

Dante surveyed the scene of the blast while still in the air. There were cars in tatters strewn around the area, damage to surrounding buildings, but seemingly no casualties or civilian injuries. He lowered himself down to street level and was met by an energy blast to the chest, sending him careening backward into a building. Bricks fell to ground from the impact and Dante shook his head to try clearing his thoughts. He couldn't see *where* the blast came from, but was fairly certain he knew *who* it came from.

A silhouette emerged in the billowing smoke coming from the burning cars, soon identifiable as Seventy-Two. "Young man, I told you that we were far from finished," he said as he jumped into the air and landed mere feet away from Dante who was still leaning against the building. Seventy-Two nodded his head at Dante, almost as if to say hello, and began punching the hero furiously. Lefts and rights landed as Dante crumpled to the ground. "Has your recent downtime made you soft, boy?" Seventy-Two asked. For a moment, the throttling nature of the blows stopped and his adversary stood up above him. Nodding his head, Seventy-Two then reached down and grabbed Dante by the ankles and swung him violently into the side of the building. The shock of the impact rocked Dante and when he hit the ground, he barely moved.

"I've been waiting for this moment, young man. I've watched you suffer through your friend's death. I let you wallow in your own self-pity just long enough for you to lose focus on me. LOOK AT ME!" Seventy-Two shouted as he noticed that Dante's head was hanging low.

Reaching down, Seventy-Two grabbed Dante by his neck and held him against the building. "Do you see me now?" he asked as he reached his right hand back and thrust it forward towards Dante's face. In that moment, Dante swung his left foot upward and made contact with Seventy-Two's groin, sending him to the ground.

"Yeah, I see you, old man," Dante replied. He swung both hands forcefully downward and made contact on Seventy-Two's back, flattening his foe. "This ends here," Dante said.

"You have that right," Seventy-Two said as he used all his might to push himself up and into Dante, sending them both launching into the air. As they continued to climb higher into the sky, they traded blows with each other. At one point, Dante could have sworn he saw blood trickling from the bottom of Seventy-Two's mask.

Weird, but it kind of makes sense. The last time he overexerted himself in New York City, he lost his abilities for a short time. Dante thought quickly. About to capitalize on this moment, he intertwined the fingers of his hands and reeled back, getting ready to strike... and then ***BOOM!***

Dante looked in the direction from which the sound had come from and saw black smoke billowing into the sky from the same area of the block party. He turned back, and Seventy-Two was gone... with no trace of the direction he took off in. That no longer mattered. Dante moved faster than he ever had, flying through the sky towards the block party, but approaching the blast made Dante feel increasingly uneasy.

He landed much faster and harder than he usually would, but he knew had to get into the party now. People were fleeing all around him. Some were covered with blood, some were carrying wounded, and others were walking away in shock. Dante passed through the gate and saw the blast impact zone. Everything felt like it was happening in slow motion at this point. Bodies were everywhere and he couldn't believe what he was seeing. Not even an hour ago, peace and joy were abounding. Off to the right of the blast zone, Dante observed Scott standing still. Their eyes met each other and Scott hurried to Dante.

"You can't go any farther," Scott said, trying to stop his friend from advancing. Shaking his head and trying to force his way past Scott, Dante began to tremble. "Don't you say it, Scott. Don't you dare say it!" Dante screamed as tears began to fall from his eyes.

Peering over his friend's shoulder, Dante could see two bodies lying underneath a black blanket. Almost nothing was identifiable, due to the covering, except for a small piece of fabric that was visible just outside. Dante fell to the ground and began to shake. He looked again, hoping that maybe his eyes were playing tricks on him. But they weren't. It was a small piece of the sunflower dress that Bethany had worn to the party.

"I'm sorry, man. They're gone. They're both gone," Scott said as he collapsed to the ground, clutching his friend tightly.

The sound of sirens filled the air and came from all directions. Ambulances, police patrol cars, fire trucks, and SWAT vehicles barreled toward the scene. Most of the event's attendees had evacuated the area by the time the first responders arrived at the scene. Smoke continued to drift upward from the smoldering crater in the ground. Many of the tents that surrounded the blast area were torn to shreds.

Several officers created a perimeter around the block party in order to keep the news crews at bay. The paramedics began tending to victims of the blast who were strewn about, both inside and outside of the gates.

A medic walked toward the blanket that was draped over Bethany and Martha and when Dante caught a glimpse of this, he screamed: *"Stay away from them!"*

Dante shoved Scott off and ran toward the two. Memories began to crash in his mind like a tsunami, and he was about to drown. Falling to the ground, visions of the time Martha slid her phone number to him, their first kiss, the proposal… He lay atop the blanket covering his girls, he left hand trembling, resting on the tiny figure of Bethany. Memories stabbed at his heart; the moment he'd held her just after she was born, his beautiful baby girl standing on his feet as they danced at the Daddy/Daughter banquet in first grade, the two of them serving food to the homeless during Thanksgiving, all rippled through his head, causing a shockwave to blast through his body.

The medic stood silently, trying to think of what his next step should be. Scott approached him and put his hand gently on his shoulder. "I got him. Just give us a minute."

Scott knelt down beside Bethany, Martha, and Dante. Fighting to hold his emotions in check, he reached his hand out and let it rest on Dante's back. Dante was still shaking as Scott moved his hands under his arms, lifted him up, and pulled him away from the scene. The medic nodded toward Scott and walked toward Bethany and Martha so he could begin his work.

Dante and Scott stopped to sit at a picnic table that was beneath a job placement tent, safely out of view of the scene that was unfolding near the blast site. "Seventy-Two was there, Scott. This wasn't him. Not directly, at least," Dante murmured. "I fought him and then when the explosion went off, he disappeared. Just vanished."

Dante wiped the tears from his eyes as Scott stood up from the table. "Whoever did this, will pay. We'll figure that out and I will make sure that it happens. Trust me,

Dante. This doesn't end here," Scott said, clenching his fists and staring off into the clouds of smoke billowing into the sky above.

Chapter Twenty-Three

Tributes to Martha and Bethany poured in from people all across the state. The work they did in the community had not gone unnoticed and now there was a large void in the heart of the city. The outside of their house was nearly overrun with balloons, flowers, and cards expressing the sorrow they felt. These items lined the walkway and covered the front porch, nearly blocking the front door, a front door which hadn't been opened since Scott brought Dante back home.

Inside the house, Dante lay on the couch and had done little more than that for just over two days. Time seemed to move by slowly for him now; the house felt too big and overwhelmingly empty. The silence within the walls of his home was deafening and the grief he felt weighed him down to the point that he was unable to function. He hadn't eaten in days and could not bring himself to. His girls had died in a blast and he couldn't do anything to stop it. And now, there he lay in darkness, in silence, in pain, alone.

The crowd outside his house stood quietly, holding candles and releasing balloons into the air in honor of Bethany and Martha. Several children who'd survived the attack and had been playing with Bethany shortly before she died were gathered outside with their parents. Two of the girls held drawings they made of Bethany in the form of an angel. They walked to the door and hung them there with tape they'd carried with them in their pocket. The girls' parents lay flowers at the doorstep and said a silent prayer before picking up their daughters.

The morning of the funeral, Scott drove to Dante's house and parked at the curb outside, just before the crowd of people. As he exited his car, the crowd separated and let him through to the front gate. "I appreciate you all for being here and wanting to show your love for Martha and Bethany, but I must ask that you leave now," Scott said sternly. "Dante needs his privacy." Memories of Steve's funeral were abounding in his head and he did not want to lash out like he did that day. Not today.

Taking note of the seriousness of his tone, the crowd disbanded and went on their way. Scott slowly paced past all of the tributes left behind. The flowers, teddy bears, balloons, and cards all seemed to be a bit too much to him, but Scott wasn't exactly exhibiting many traits of sympathy or empathy lately. Except today, today was different. His family was in tatters and he had to try to make his way through the ruins to collect what was left of Dante.

He reached out, grasped the doorknob, and turned it, surprised to find that the door had remained unlocked since the day he'd helped Dante into the house. All of the lights inside were off, but thankfully, there was enough daylight coming in through the windows to illuminate the first floor of the house. Scott noticed that Dante was lying on the couch, but he continued on toward the kitchen where he grabbed a glass and filled it up with water from the refrigerator. He quietly approached the couch and sat down on the coffee table in front of it. Dante continued to lie there in a deep sleep. Snoring. Scott hated snoring.

Scott thrust the glass of water forward and the water splashed off of Dante's face, causing Dante to spring up in shock. "Oh, hey there, Dante. Time to wake up," Scott said as he and Dante began laughing. This was the first interaction Dante had had with a person in days, and it felt good. Scott used to wake Dante up this way when they roomed together, several years before he'd met Martha. Dante hated it, but played along since Scott seemed to get a kick out of it. The two, almost in sync with their thoughts, began to reminisce about the simpler times that seemed to be so far away now.

Scott reached into the closet and grabbed the suit he'd left for his friend the morning after he'd brought him back home. "Let's get you dressed, big fella. I know that you don't want to, but…"

"I have to," Dante interrupted. Dante took the suit and went into the bathroom to get himself ready. Still sitting on the table, Scott looked around and couldn't help but feel overcome by emotion when he saw all of the portraits of Dante, Martha, and Bethany. Baby pictures and family photographs adorned the walls and the mantle above the fireplace.

Dante emerged from the bathroom, but Scott did not move. He walked up behind his friend and put his hand on his shoulder, resulting in Scott nearly jumping out of his skin. The look in Scott's eyes was indescribable. It was almost like he'd seen a ghost.

"Come on, man. We have to go," Dante said, walking toward the door and holding it open for Scott. As he shut the door, his eyes locked on the drawings that were taped there. He grabbed them and the teddy bears that were on the porch below him and continued his trek to the car.

As the two arrived at the cemetery, they both noticed that there were no reporters in attendance, which Scott delighted in. Today was about their families and friends. Not headlines. Dante and Scott walked to the front row and sat down beside Martha's parents. Martha's mother reached out and grabbed onto Dante's hand, looked at him with tears in his eyes, and then looked ahead at the caskets holding her daughter and granddaughter.

The pastor delivered his message and closed with a prayer before asking if anyone else had anything they would like to say. Releasing himself from the grip of Martha's mother's hand, Dante stood up and walked to the podium. He placed the pictures and teddy bears on top, and, for a moment, he stood there silently. His eyes glancing over at the caskets before him, he removed his sunglasses and began to speak.

"This is by far the most difficult day of my life. I am standing here in an unimaginable circumstance, speaking at my wife and daughter's funeral. I always thought that they would be the ones to bury me, based on my occupation alone. But here we are. Martha was a gift from above. A sentiment that her parents could testify to from the moment they laid eyes on her. She had a heart the size of Los Angeles and wanted the best for everyone around her. Her heart is what initially drew me to her. And if I'm being honest, I loved her from the moment I laid eyes on her too. She was a beacon of hope and light that shone too brightly for this world," Dante said as he began to tremble.

"And Bethany... oh my sweet Bethany. Your light was dimmed much too soon. Your love and genuine compassion for others was far beyond that of which I had seen in people many years your senior. Being your Daddy was the greatest gift I had ever been given, and now I'm not sure what I will do. I know that I failed you both and that is a pain that I don't know if I can carry. My heart is broken, as are all of yours. I thought I was doing the right thing, but I should have never left you alone. But that brought us here. And I won't allow it to happen again. I lost my heart and my sunshine. This is the end of the Special Forces," Dante said with tears in his eyes.

Walking from around the podium, he stopped at Martha's casket and placed roses on top of it before bowing his head for a moment to pray. Then, he walked over to Bethany's casket and stood still. He placed the pictures and teddy bears from the porch on top and fell to the ground. The pain was too much to take; his body could not withstand it any longer.

Scott quickly leapt from his seat and rushed to Dante's side. He knelt there beside him and wrapped his arms around his friend as they both began crying. Silence overtook the cemetery for a few moments and the two stood up together. Dante brushed himself off and straightened his jacket before putting his sunglasses back on. Without saying another word, he looked at Scott and placed his hand on his friend's heart before taking a few steps in the opposite direction and then launching himself into the air. Scott stood beside Martha and Bethany's caskets knowing that Special Forces was gone, and now the world would change forever.

Chapter Twenty-Four

"Hello and thank you for tuning in to WGKB 24's Five O'clock News. I'm Charli Hernandez and as always, I'm joined by Marshall Orlando. Violent crime has increased exponentially since the group of extraordinary people known as 'Special Forces' disbanded. Bank robberies, assaults, and murders have seen a double-digit increase and the previously touted decline in gang activity has since begun to rise. In related news, we will have an expert on tonight's 10pm broadcast who will expound on the impact that the Special Forces had on the community as well as the world, the disappearance of Dante, Scott, and oddly enough, the menacing Seventy-Two."

"That's right Charli, crime in Los Angeles and around the country has begun to skyrocket in the absence of the Specials," Marshall said as he stood up from behind the news desk and slowly walked toward a screen located to the right of the anchor's seat. "What is even more troubling is that crime is at levels that dwarf the Pre-Specials era," he continued, pointing to a series of graphs illustrating the increase he and his co-anchor were describing.

"Be sure to tune in later tonight for what promises to be an earth-shattering take on the current state of the world and what may have been happening with the Specials all along," Charli said in closing.

In the abandoned warehouse that he was now calling home, Seventy-Two stood in a darkened corner, staring into what was remaining of an all but shattered mirror leaning up against the wall. He rested his left hand on the wall and leaned closer to his reflection, running his right hand along his face.

"Time's not been too kind to you has it?" he asked, inching even closer to the glass and almost expecting a reply.

"No, I guess it hasn't," replied a deeper voice, one that he could not place but felt a sense of familiarity. "But we have had our fun along the way, haven't we?".

Grinning widely, Seventy-Two pushed back off of the wall to help stabilize himself. "We sure did. Hell, it's been a blast," he said laughing.

"Well, the time for fun is over! We have played this game for too long. Chess not checkers, right? I think it's time for check mate. The end-game. They are reeling, and we are sitting in a warehouse chatting? You're better than this, and you know it," the voice continued.

The smile faded from his face as he turned his back on the mirror. Bending down, he picked up a stone from the ground and stared at it. In a sudden motion, he spun around and launched the stone at the mirror. As the glass splintered, exploding into tiny shards, the sound of laughter began to emanate from all around him. The noise echoed down the dark corridors and bounced off the walls in each room of the hollow warehouse that housed Seventy-Two. The laughter's volume increased, causing the few remaining windows to tremble, and then there was silence.

Seventy-Two stood in the center of the room alone, shaken, and baffled by what he just witnessed. There were times in the recent past in which he'd felt a presence nearby that was neither his compatriots nor himself. He had been alone for quite some time or so he had thought. Wiping his eyes vigorously and trying to regain some semblance of clarity, he shook his head. He began to feel an increased concern that he was spiraling out of control. When he'd started his mission he was focused, organized, diligent in his approach to serving his brand of justice. Now, he felt the way he was going about his mission was erratic at best. His attacks were few and far between and seemed to be lacking a sincere motivation.

That is until the event that led to the deaths of Martha, Bethany, and many other innocent bystanders. He felt a swelling sense of pride with that one. A lot of time went into devising the plan that rocked Los Angeles to its core and ultimately resulted in the disappearance of the heroes that had come to be admired by the city and the world collectively.

But now what? he thought. *Where is there to go from here?* The attack has caused Dante to go into isolation, whereabouts unknown.

The sound of a slow and deliberate pace of footsteps began to fill the silent void that had been there since the laughter ceased. "Hello?" Seventy-Two called out, staring toward the doorframe at the other side of the room. The warehouse was dimly lit by candles that had been spread out intentionally by Seventy-Two to allow just enough light that doorways could be illuminated. "Who's there?" he called out again.

Suddenly, the sound of footsteps came to a halt and there was nothingness in the air again. Growing more concerned, Seventy-Two began to move toward the direction of the footsteps. A powerful gust of wind burst through the opening, extinguishing the flames on every candle and knocking Seventy-Two backwards.

"I had always hoped it was you," said the person in the doorway. "I had a feeling, but I had to be sure. I understand why you couldn't tell me who you were in the

beginning, but what I can't understand is why you wouldn't

tell me as we started to work together. I'm patient; I've waited

a long time for this moment, so I'll forgive that transgression. I

have done everything you have asked to this point, following

your orders like a good soldier. However, I can no longer stand

idly by while you lose control. You need to refocus your

energy on returning to a position of power. And I can help you

with that, if you'll let me."

Reluctantly, Seventy-Two nodded in

agreement. "We have done so much to this point. We are

almost at the end of phase-one. Let's do this together...how it

always should have been."

"Charli Hernandez here, reporting from South Hill

Street Los Angeles. Reports came in waves regarding potential

criminal activity at Perch, the popular rooftop restaurant that

has been played host to reported mob meetings," she said,

standing in front of a camera which was aimed at an angle

that focused on her face while showing the restaurant off in the distance.

The normal ambience of a bustling area in the city was soon shattered by the sounds of police sirens as vehicles sped to the scene and came to a screeching halt at the curb outside the restaurant. Police helicopters then closed in and circled the building. The news crew moved in and was met quickly by officers who were setting up a perimeter around the area.

As the officers directed Charli and her crew to step back, an explosion rocked the rooftop restaurant. Charli took off running to the news van, but her cameraman refused to let this story go undocumented. *The people would need to see this*, he thought. This wasn't normal criminal activity; there was much more to it than that.

He maneuvered himself around the barricade that had been set up by the police just moments earlier. He thought to himself that this scene was beginning to become eerily reminiscent of the New York City attack launched by

Seventy-Two. *KABLOOM!* Another blast rocked a building on the other side of the street, and, just like that, he had two scenes to try capturing on film.

Bricks and other debris fell from the buildings and toward the sidewalk below. The officers began shouting at the civilians ahead of them to get out of the way. At just the right moment, a couple who'd been walking casually together ran off of the sidewalk, and seconds later a large piece of the building crashed where they had been mere moments before. The cameraman continued to run toward the buildings as others were running in the opposite direction.

He slid on the ground and crouched down beside a car parked outside of the restaurant. Focusing his camera upward, he tightened the shot he had on the building and was able to make out a small group, no more than six, standing together and emerging from the flames that were shooting out of the blast site. They appeared to be wearing military grade armor complete with helmets and automatic rifles. One of the members of the group reached to his back and pulled out a compact weapon, one that the cameraman could not identify which was worrisome to him because he had seen plenty weapons and artillery from covering the city as well as war zones across the world.

A police helicopter changed its direction slightly, allowing one of the officers to get a clear shot of the group on the roof. It didn't seem like there were any civilian survivors which must have been why the officers had their weapons trained on the group standing there. "Damn, why'd he hesitate?" the cameraman whispered to himself. He zoomed in tighter and was able to get a clear view of the man as he pulled the trigger, sending a blinding blast of energy from the weapon he held to the helicopter. Once the blast made contact, there was a moment when nothing happened, but that was followed by a violent explosion that engulfed the helicopter in flames and launched the officers into the air.

He panned his view out, and, while he wasn't happy about capturing the moment that the officers were plummeting through the air, he felt that it was his responsibility to keep rolling. As the officers closed in on the street below, something flew through the air and caught them an instant before they met their demise. "Dante," the cameraman whispered.

The officers were set down beside the patrol car down the block and they shook hands with the man who'd saved them. He turned around and looked back up as what remained of the helicopter began to barrel towards another building. He launched himself into the air, and his speed increased rapidly. As he ascended, he could hear screams, see flames, and smell death with each passing moment. He closed in on the helicopter and grabbed ahold of it, not slowing down, and certainly not as gracefully as he had seen Dante perform in the past. Once he cleared the surrounding buildings, he tossed the helicopter into the air, leaned back, and shot a blast of energy from his chest that tore the uniform he was wearing and incinerated its target upon impact.

The civilians below erupted in applause. The cameraman wasn't so quick to jump to his feet in adulation for what he just witnessed because something felt off to him. He kept his focus on the person he'd initially thought was Dante, only to find that it was not. It was someone else entirely.

The Special who was hovering in the air above the city turned around slowly and began to move toward the rooftop where the attack had been launched. As he closed in on the group, who had their weapons aimed in his direction, he smiled. The cameraman caught that smile. "He's enjoying this," he murmured quietly. The six military fatigue-clad individuals stood shoulder to shoulder and began to fire on their target. The cameraman was sure he was capturing the death of a Special, and he was worried. The city couldn't take another loss of that magnitude. They needed hope.

And then there was laughter. A menacing, worrying laughter. The Special took all that had been fired his way and he just laughed. The cameraman quickly became unsettled and that feeling was multiplied when he saw the Special extend his arms in front of him. The Special then separated his arms and brought his hands back together. As his hands made contact, a wave of energy burst toward the rooftop and the people who had launched the assault disintegrated on impact.

The applause that was coming from the street below was quickly replaced by screams of horror. The Special lowered himself to the ground and came to rest beside the cameraman. The cameraman was fighting off shock as he tried to focus his camera upward revealing that it was Scott, not Dante, who was standing in front of him.

"Why?" asked the cameraman as he lifted himself from the ground.

"*Why?* Do you disagree with my method?" Scott asked quizzically. "My method stopped the attacks and saved countless lives, yet you have the audacity to question it. Would you prefer that I took Dante's tried and true approach of using peace to disarm these types of situations? How many people died as a result of that approach?" Scott shouted.

He seemed to be getting increasingly more frustrated as moments ticked past. "You want to know why? *You want to know why!* The world has changed. That's why."

Chapter Twenty-Five

In a brightly lit studio, several panelists gathered together at a round table to discuss the return of one part of the Special Forces and his response to the attack that claimed thirty-two lives including the lives of the group of attackers who vaulted Scott back into the spotlight.

The terrifying display of aggression and lack of remorse had shocked onlookers to their core. Paul Richardson, anchor of Major Headline News or MHN, sat at the head of the table. The smirk on his face indicated that he was reveling in his moderator role. The remaining news media members at the table represented a collection of local news personalities, all gathered to share their opinions on the events that had transpired in broad daylight. From the brazen attack to the cold and swift response.

Staring directly into the camera, Richardson straightened his silk tie and cleared his throat. "Ladies and gentlemen, we are coming to you live from Los Angeles. I am surrounded by a group of the most respected reporters in the area to dive deeper into the return of the Specials and the

horrifying actions of Scott, better known as Flight. I know that

this channel typically allows callers to chime in with their

opinions, but the due to the volatility of tonight's topic, we

will not be fielding any calls from viewers," he said as he

squirmed anxiously in his chair.

Raising his left hand, signaling the production

crew to begin playing the footage he had gathered, Paul

Richardson flashed an odd, slightly disturbing smile and slowly

lowered his hand. The footage that played on the screens

behind him showed the moment when Scott emerged to take

on the attackers, when he saved the officer from imminent

death, and when he killed the attackers in cold blood.

"Now, I'll start this discussion off by asking

you… is this what you would call a hero?" Richardson asked

the panel. Just as Lucas James, Editor in Chief at the Los

Angeles Times began to respond, Richardson held up his hand.

"You bet your ass that this is not a hero. At

least not in the traditional sense of the word. This is, in fact, what this city no the world needs right now. The world needs someone to stand up for those suffering from injustices. While he may not represent what the world has come to know and define as a hero, he represents the future. And by God, ladies and gentlemen, the future is bright."

"How can you possibly sit there and say that this type of 'justice' is what the world needs right now, Paul?" asked James Madison, renowned field reporter who had covered wars in foreign countries and famine across the world. "If this was any other civilian taking matters into their own hands, we'd have a manhunt on our hands. But just because this person represents an all but forgotten group of vigilantes, we should just turn a blind eye to the brutal way in which he handled the situation?"

Visibly irritated, Paul leaned in and rested his elbows on the desk in front of him. He reached into his shirt pocket and grabbed a silk handkerchief and dabbed the sweat that was beading up on his forehead. "A 'blind eye' you say.

Isn't that what everyone's favorite hero Dante has turned on these events? A 'blind eye' shit," Paul continued.

The show's producer angrily leapt up from his chair and began flailing his hands in the air to signal that Paul needed to watch the type of language he used on the broadcast. Paul responded by raising his middle finger up high above his head. "Ladies and gentlemen, what we have here is a failure to come to a mutual understanding. The world needs more people, Specials, hell...the world needs anyone willing to step up and respond to those who look to harm or oppress those too weak to stand up for themselves. That's what Scott did. He saved countless lives by taking the action he took," Paul said as he stood up from his seat.

The other panelists sat silently, almost in shock at what was unfolding in front of them. The images on the screens shifted from the recent attack to past events focused on Dante's brand of heroism and his battles with Seventy-Two. The faint sound of a telephone ringing began to emerge and Paul reached into his pockets, clumsily grabbing his phone and silencing the call.

"Heh... sorry about that folks. I know that we said we wouldn't take any calls on tonight's show, but some people just won't take a hint," he said. "I think it's time to end this charade, folks. I know that *I'm* tired of Paul's shit; our dear viewers absolutely have to have hit their limit with this guy. I mean, I can barely stand him and I'm the one projecting his image," Paul said as his appearance began to change slowly to eventually reveal a laughing Seventy-Two.

Terrified, the panelists jumped from their seats and began to run toward the emergency exit off of the left side of the stage. The sound of laughter came to an immediate halt as Seventy-Two launched an energy blast toward the ceiling above the door, causing rubble to pile high in front of the exit. "Where's everyone going? I thought we were having good conversation?" Seventy-Two said with a frightening tone.

"Conversation? It was a more like a one man show tonight, asshole," replied James Madison.

"Point well taken, Jim. However, there are times when one must conversate with oneself in order to make the most sense of a situation. I mean, how far would you and I get in a discussion before I got bored with your small-minded point of view?" Seventy-Two said, standing below a stage light that had shaken loose from the blast he caused.

Taking notice of the light dangling above his head, Seventy-Two raised his right hand and quickly maneuvered it in the direction of the reporters and broadcasters gathered by the door. With that motion, the stage light ripped from the structure above him and flew rapidly toward James Madison, ultimately crashing into his head, sending the reporter crumbling to the ground and the others scattering throughout the studio.

Seventy-Two's phone began to ring again, and he shifted his focus from the remaining panelists and looked into the camera, which was still recording. "Ladies and gentlemen, it would appear as if we have a caller that has yet to take the HINT!" he said as he angrily ripped the phone from the pouch affixed to his right leg and placed it against his right ear.

"Yes?!?" he shouted. "Really? Ok, fine," Seventy-Two said abruptly. "Well folks, it looks like the police have surrounded the building and are closing in on this very studio. What am I to do now?" he said sarcastically as he paced back and forth, dragging the camera with him. Stopping suddenly, he raised the camera up and brought the lens close to his face. "Dante, this is all for you, boy," he said, placing the camera down at his feet, giving view to the devastation behind him.

The police officers spread out and stood on either side of the door to the studio that was broadcasting this terrible takeover of sorts. One officer signaled to the others and he forcefully kicked the door open and they all made their way into the room, stopping short of Seventy-Two who was standing in the center of the producer's area.

"I'm glad you were all able to make it to today's meeting," Seventy-Two said, chuckling as he burst into a ball of fire, emitting energy blasts in every direction. The blasts blew through the equipment, from the tables to the recording devices set up throughout the room - it all went up in flames. Officers were quickly engulfed in flames as Seventy-Two ascended through the ceiling and burst through the rooftop as the fire and destruction followed him.

"Where is he?!?" shouted Seventy-Two, high above the television studio he had just decimated. "Dante! I know you're out there somewhere!" he continued shouting maniacally while he recklessly fired energy blasts at nearby buildings. Slowing his spin to a stop, he noticed military personnel approaching the scene, and Seventy-Two disappeared quickly. He didn't fly away, he didn't run...he just disappeared, leaving devastation in his wake.

"Are there any heroes left?" mumbled those left behind. "Where is Dante?"

Chapter Twenty-Six

As reports of the attack in the news studio began to make their way through national and international media outlets, Los Angeles came to a standstill. The city had been at the epicenter of the Specials shockwaves that were getting progressively worse as the years went by. Citizens of the surrounding area began to feel less safe as the uncertainty of their security continued to rise. Many took to the streets to take part in peaceful demonstrations, similar to those from years before when Dante had first appeared. Others gathered in massive groups and stormed the streets in aggressive and violent demonstrations.

Where there would typically be a smattering of reporters set up in the area to get footage of the protests or quotes from those taking part in them, there was a minimal presence. Most local news channels used drones to capture the footage and newly set up toll-free call centers to interview witnesses or participants. Things were changing, and fear had begun to sweep the nation.

A new and concerning trend began to emerge during the turbulent reaction to the most recent attack by Seventy-Two. Information began to leak to the public and to the anti-Special hate groups regarding the whereabouts of individuals who were being monitored as "Assumed Specials".

One of the groups, known as the Coalition for Human Advancement, was rumored to be in the process of gathering and detaining the individuals identified in the leaked records. Most disturbing of these events was footage that was anonymously sent to Charli Hernandez of WGKB-24. Going against the directive given by her superiors, Charli sat alone at the anchor desk and looked ahead into the camera with what could best be described as a vacant stare.

"Thank you for joining WGKB-24 Headline News, I'm Charli Hernandez and I am tasked with the...unfortunate responsibility of bringing you updates this evening. We have witnessed many despicable events over the last few years. And if we're being honest, many of us became numb to the seemingly senseless acts of violence being played out across the country."

Shifting slightly in her chair, Charli changed her focus to a camera to the right of the set. Before continuing, she lowered her head, wiped a tear from her left eye, and looked to the camera again.

"Months ago, Dante's wife and young daughter were murdered in an attack at an event that the hero, his family, and friends had put together to benefit the community. Not just the Specials community, the entire community. Yet, hate and death followed them there. The villain known as Seventy-Two has gone on to carry out unprecedented assaults in hopes of bringing down the establishment that caused him harm and which continues to persecute others like him. Let us not forget that he was held captive by the very government that is sworn to protect its citizens...of all races, creeds, and religions."

"I want to make one thing clear. I am not a sympathizer as it relates to Seventy-Two and his actions. I'm just saying that we should not lose sight of what started this," she said as she signaled to the producer in the track to prep the video to be played for the audience.

"I offer you this disclaimer. The video that I am about to play is graphic and violent in nature. Other networks refuse to play it, much less report on the contents of it, but I will not refuse. This is my responsibility. I know that it may cost me my job, but that's a price I am willing to pay," she concluded as she gave the producer the cue to play the video.

What happened next would later be described as a shift in the Human/Special Civil War that had only just begun. The footage was shaky and seemed to be recorded on a cellphone. The person recording was sitting inside a vehicle occupied by three others wearing military garb and clutching a variety of weapons. The audio was muffled because of the way the person was holding the phone, but dialogue could be heard once the volume was adjusted.

The four men exited the vehicle and knelt down close together under the protection of the night. "No one is chickening out at this point, right?" one man said as the other three confirmed. "Good," he replied as he cocked his weapon.

The group walked toward a house that looked like it was located at the end of a cul-de-sac. One of the men fidgeted with a device that caused a short in the electricity and then suddenly, the power was out. The footage shifted to a camera that was mounted on the shirt of one of the men. The men approached the house and split up into different directions. Two went to the front door and the others went to opposite sides of the exterior of the house.

As they pounded on the door, a light could be seen through the windows on the front porch. A man holding a flashlight opened the door and was immediately shot by the two attackers. He fell to the ground, clutching the wound on his chest, which was bleeding heavily. "How...baby, run!" he tried screaming as loud as he could, but his voice came out nothing more than a whisper.

"How? Easy, friend. I have the secret to your "invincibility." We've been working on weaponry that could neutralize your kind from the beginning. Have you ever bled

before this moment?" the attacker asked provokingly. "And

don't you worry, we'll take good care of your daughter," he

said before snapping the man's neck and moving into the

house.

The pair still on the perimeter made it through

windows on either side and stood in the living room where the

others met them. "You know what we're here to do… specific

orders," he said as the audio began to become increasingly

distorted.

"Daddy!" screamed a young lady, who was no

older than nineteen. She ran down the stairs from her

bedroom and went toward the front door when she saw him

her father, lying in a pool of his own blood in the doorway.

Almost in shock, the men stood in awe, as if they could not

believe that their prey had presented herself so easily. Two of

them quietly advanced, clutching a net that had currents of

electricity rippling through it.

In an instant, the girl spun around and stared at the attackers, her red hair swirling from the breeze blowing in through the front door. With a flick of her wrist, the net wrapped around the two men and the electricity increased, killing them almost immediately.

"Get that bitch!" screamed the man with the camera attached to his jacket. The attacker who'd shot her father stood there with his gun aimed at her, his target illuminated by the sight dot in the center of her forehead. With another gentle movement of her hand, the attacker turned his gun on himself and fired, sending him to the ground in a heap.

The other attacker lowered his weapons and dropped to his knees. With a menacing grin on her face, the girl walked toward him and rested her hand on his head.

"I... I... this is all being recorded," he said with a shaky voice and as his body trembled.

"Good," she replied. "I'd hate to forget what I did to the assholes who broke into my home and killed my father in front of me. Why would you bring this battle to our doorstep?" she asked as she began to levitate before her would-be killer.

"Who are you?" the man asked, his voice trembling.

"Who am I? That's an awfully funny thing to come from the man who came here to kill me," she replied as her eyes reddened and fire appeared from her hands. "My name is Amelia. However, you can call me Blaze," she said as she thrust her hands forward, blasting a flame through the man who was kneeling before her. As the first flames made impact, she raised one of her hands and the camera detached from his shirt as he writhed on the ground screaming, engulfed in flames.

The camera was still functioning as she looked directly into it. "If it is a war you're looking for, you found it. Just be careful what you wish for. Because you are going to get it and then some," she said as she threw the camera through the front door and into the street.

The video ended and Charli looked into the camera, visibly exhausted. "Welp. There goes my career. And I'm totally fine with it. There are men out there who are part of the Coalition for Human Advancement that are willing to decimate entire families, including children...*children*. Are these the people you want standing up for you? Are these the type of people you want to rally around? We must now decide which side of this war we are on, because, ladies and gentlemen, the war is here. And it is only going to get much worse," Charli said before vanishing from sight. "We are everywhere," she concluded as the broadcast went off of the air.

Chapter Twenty-Seven

An elevated feeling of panic spread quickly after Charli Hernandez's shocking revelation following the graphic attack and attempted abduction at the hands of the Coalition for Human Advancement. The rate of Specials who came out of hiding following the bold declaration of war by a young woman who had lost her father increased exponentially and the world was not ready.

Some gathered in the name of peace, and others... well, others gathered with more devious intentions. The Disciples of Dante, a mixture of humans and peaceful Specials, marched on Washington and various other points of political importance. Conversely, an unnamed group of Specials clashed directly with human aggressors who showed zero compassion or interest in coexisting with their kind.

The war was here, and Dante remained silent and isolated from the public eye. The house that he called home with Martha and Bethany stood empty. Reports and grainy video featuring sightings of Dante emerged slowly as the civil war was in its infancy. When approached for comment about the videos, showing Dante frequenting liquor stores and staggering to and from a rundown apartment building, Scott brushed the questions aside.

"I haven't seen Dante since...since the funeral. I've called, texted, and got nothing in response. We were like brothers...hell, we are brothers. I love that man and hope he is doing okay. However, one thing I won't do is stand here and speculate for the media on his mental or physical state," Scott said before abruptly launching himself into the air, away from the very questions he was asking himself more often than he'd care to admit.

Can't be him. It just can't, Scott thought while sitting on the edge of a rooftop overlooking one of his and Dante's favorite places to drive when they were younger, the Sunset Strip. "We need you, man," he said softly.

"Need who?" Scott leapt to his feet and spun around coming face to face with Seventy-Two. "Dante? You *need* Dante?" he asked with a disturbing grin on his face.

"What could he possibly do for you? He couldn't even protect his wife and daughter," he continued just as Scott thrust both of his fists into Seventy-Two's stomach, sending him hurtling backward into an HVAC unit atop the roof. "Shit, I'm outta here!" screamed a man clutching a camera close to his chest and running to the door which led to the stairwell.

Jumping over debris, Scott closed in on his nemesis rapidly. As he got closer to his target, he pulled his right hand back then connected hard with Seventy-Two's jaw, causing his adversary to stumble backward.

"You son of a bitch!" Scott shouted, lifting up a piece of the rubble that had fallen loose. Holding it high, Scott looked down on his rival and paused for a moment. His delay lasted just long enough for Seventy-Two to fire an energy blast at Scott. A burning sensation shot through his shoulder as he reached for the ghastly wound. The piece of cement that fell as a result was now at eye level and Seventy-Two jumped into the air and kicked it right into Scott's face. Scott fell to the ground and did not move.

"Boy, this didn't have to go this way. I think you know that," Seventy-Two said before pausing. He felt an intense heat behind him and he reluctantly turned around. Just as Scott was surprised by Seventy-Two on the roof with him, Seventy-Two turned to find that Amelia... Blaze, was before him. For a moment, she just hovered there. Clad in an orange and red uniform with flame patterned trimmings, she hovered above the rooftop with her hands emitting flames which were being expelled with such force that they allowed her to stay in the air.

"Boys, boys, boys... is this the best way for us to use our powers? I think there are plenty of other outlets that we could expend our energy, but hey...why not fight each other in the most cliché hero/villain way possible, right?" Blaze said chuckling.

"He started it," Scott replied sullenly, causing Seventy-Two and Blaze to lower their heads in unison. Without further hesitation, Seventy-Two reached back to fire another energy blast, but Scott was... gone. Just gone.

"So, you're the big bad wolf, huh?" Blaze asked, looking Seventy-Two up and down. "You don't seem so bad. Just old, gray, and cranky."

"Young lady, I have tried to be patient with you, but you are pushing the limits of my tolerance. What in the hell do you want?" Seventy-Two asked angrily.

"Um... I think I want exactly what you want, pops. I want revenge. I want to make them pay, and I want them to pay now," Blaze replied.

"Well, you came to the right person. I specialize in revenge. It's sort of my th..."

In rapid succession, the flames that were holding Blaze aloft flashed in front of Seventy-Two's face, just close enough to distract him, and were quickly followed by several stiff jabs, sending him to the ground. Without letting up, she reached down and grasped onto his neck, lifting him high above her head. "I guess I should've been a little more specific. You're included in the 'them' of my previous statement. I'm starting with you," she said sternly.

"But why? Aren't we the same?" Seventy-Two said.

"We're nowhere near the same. You're sloppy... and weak. You can't even sustain your powers for long anymore. But don't worry... I hear it happens to people your age," she said before bursting into laughter.

"You're sick! What do you hope to get from this encounter? You're certainly not going to kill me. Many have tried before you, little girl. I will be here long after you are gone," Seventy-Two said confidently.

"No, I won't kill you. Upon further review... and as much as I hate to admit it, you could prove to be very helpful. I need you to help me bring him back."

"Who? Dante? You want that pathetic loser back? He's long gone. It's people like us versus the rest of the world, dear. Haven't you seen the news lately? There's a bit of a civil war going on right now."

"Yeah, I've seen it. But not on the news... gosh, you really are old," Blaze said with a tinge of sarcasm that nearly sent Seventy-Two into a fit of rage.

"Oh, my G... you're truly insufferable. Has anyone ever told you that?" he asked.

"Eh...once or twice. But, I'm effective. And to be completely honest with you, I'm sick of waiting. I meant it when I said I that they found the war they were looking for. It's time for us to band together and show them who is truly atop the food chain now."

Blaze levitated again, aided by the fire bursting from her hands and then she turned to gaze out toward the Sunset Strip. "He always said that he wanted to change the world, right? Well, the world has changed, and we are going to be taking the battle to the very people who looked to rid the world of us. However, we won't be the ones who go into hiding. We won't turn our back on this fight. We will lead others like us into battle. And we will win," Blaze said before taking off into the sky.

Chapter Twenty-Eight

The sun had barely crept up over the horizon, but he had already been lying there awake for hours. He spent some of this time listening to the occasional car drive by outside or the isolated hoot of an owl. However, when he couldn't stay asleep and it was silent outside, he found himself watching the love of his life sleep peacefully. And he took solace in knowing that he was one of the contributing factors to this peace being prevalent in their household. They didn't live away from the public, they lived on a crowded street, their house about twenty feet away from their neighbors'.

There was a wonderful feeling of serenity in their lives, but his mind just could not stop racing. It was almost as if he could not accept that this feeling could be permanent. His own personal history tended to cause him to feel that times like this were fleeting. So even in the face of all of this, he would lie there and watch her as she slept. *This is what home should feel like*, he would think.

As the sun began to rise higher into the sky, the room began to get brighter. *Bethany would surely be awake soon*, he thought before his mind drifted off to fond memories he held close to his heart. It was almost poetic that Bethany crossed his mind just as the sun brought light to the room. He always said that she was his sunshine and that she brought light to his life.

She always laughed at his dad jokes. "Oh, daaaaaaad," she would say, almost embarrassed by how much love he was showering her with...or at least that is how he chose to look at it. In reality, she was probably just embarrassed by her dad being... well, her dad.

Martha was lying on her side, facing Dante's side of the bed with the sun shining on her face. He couldn't help but smile. *Man, she's beautiful*, he thought to himself as he continued to gaze lovingly at his wife. And almost as if she could hear his thoughts, she smiled and he brushed the hair away from her eyes.

"Hey, gorgeous," he said gently. She stretched and let out a long yawn, covering her face with both of her hands.

"Hey, handsome," she replied sleepily, remnants of her smile on her face.

"What time is it?" she asked.

"Seven," he replied. Quickly, Martha brushed off the blankets and then rushed over to her closet. "You don't really have to go to work; I think you could take today off," Dante said from the bed.

"Yeah, but there's so much to do. Plus, you'll probably have to go save the world at some point soon anyway. Evil doesn't sleep in!" she said with a deep belly laugh.

"Real funny," Dante replied as he allowed his body to rise up from the bed and float softly to the closet. "Besides, can you really leave *this*?" He said flexing his muscles.

"Daddy?" Bethany said softly as she entered their bedroom.

"Intruder!" Dante shouted as he shifted his focus to the sleepy beauty. He flew over quickly and scooped her up into his arms. "Oh no! She's got me!" he shouted as he wrapped her arms around his neck and he flew backwards to the bed, landing on top of the pile of blankets.

"Thankfully, I was saved by this cushy pile of blankets," he continued in an overly dramatic voice that always elicited a burst of laughter from Bethany.

Bethany looked toward the pillows at the head of the bed and began to make her move. "Anything but the pillows!" Dante bellowed, still employing the drama-filled voice.

Chuckling, Bethany clutched one of the pillows and swung it at Dante, connecting with his left shoulder. With a look of shock on his face, Dante glanced down to his arm and then back at Bethany. "I never thought that it would be my own daughter...my own blood, who would take me down.

And with a fluffy pillow at that," he said as he slowly rolled from the bed to the floor.

Seeing that her window of opportunity had opened and now was the time to attack, Bethany was faced with a decision to make: leave Dante lying there to lick his wounds and come back for more at a later time, or pounce and remove that scenario from the equation.

Relentlessly, she chose the latter and pounced from atop the bed, falling with force and landing on Dante's stomach. Dramatically, as was most of his behavior during this brutal bout, Dante's tongue exited his mouth and his eyes closed.

"One, two, three!" Bethany shouted as she pinned her father in a way that would make most professional wrestlers jealous. She then stood up beside her father and raised her hands victoriously.

"Ladies and gentlemen, your winner... Battling Bethany!" Martha chimed in as she exited the closet, fully dressed in one of her favorite business suits. Bethany bowed to her left and right as Martha held her hand high. Martha

looked down at her husband and smiled. "You fought

valiantly, Dante. This opponent was just too much for you to

overcome," she said in an exaggerated sportscaster's play-by-

play voice.

Dante opened his eyes and they made contact

with Martha's for only a few seconds. Dante always gushed on

his wife and would tell his friends, and anyone that would

listen, that he felt like he could get lost in her eyes for

lifetimes.

Flashing a sly grin, he sat up and wrapped his

arms around Bethany. "You're mine now!" he said, laughing

maniacally before he lifted her into the air and flew in circles

above the bed.

"Well then...breakfast?" Martha asked.

"Breakfast!" Dante and Bethany gleefully shouted in

unison.

"Breakfast it is then." Martha grabbed her purse from

beside the nightstand and exited the bedroom.

Dante put the TV on for Bethany while he took a shower. *This is the* life, he thought as the water showered onto his head. The lights in the bathroom flickered off and on and the water temperature got increasingly colder the longer the lights malfunctioned. "Bethany!" Dante yelled from the shower. But there was no response. Dante's mind quickly went into worst case scenario mode and he rushed out of the shower, wrapped a towel around his waist and entered the bedroom.

"Bethany!" he shouted again. The television was off and the sun that was once coming into the room was covered up by dark storm clouds that must have moved in while he was in the shower. He peered out into the hallway and the lights were off out there as well. "Bethany! Where are you, honey?!?"

Dante ran quickly into the closet and put on the suit that had become synonymous with his superhero crusade. Clad in the uniform that many had become so familiar with, he ran from the bedroom and skipped the stairs, instead settling on jumping from the second floor to the corridor below. He hurriedly ran to the kitchen only to see an empty frying pan on the stovetop and place settings at the table with three chairs pulled out.

"Bethany… Martha!" he shouted again as he felt a hand on his right shoulder. "Baby, we're right here," Martha said. Dante looked into her eyes, almost as if he had seen a ghost. He wrapped his arms around her and hugged her tightly. "Easy, Slugger… don't squeeze too tight. I'm only human, you know," she said.

She put both hands on his chest and leaned in closely. He looked at her and rested his forehead on hers, becoming one with her for a brief moment in time. Dante turned around quickly and saw Bethany sitting at the table, shoveling the scrambled eggs that Martha made into her mouth. He almost couldn't believe his eyes. They weren't there just a moment ago…and the sun was now shining again.

"There's a plate and glass of milk on the counter for you, baby. I'm going to take Bethany with me. You get some rest, okay?" Martha said, walking over to Bethany.

Bethany stood up from the chair, dressed in her favorite

sunflower print dress.

"Yeah, daddy. We're gonna get going now. Love

you," she said in voice that seemed too mature for her age.

"You don't really have to go...you know that,

right?" Dante asked with a voice closer to a whisper.

"No, baby. We do have to go. You have work to

do...you're not finished yet. We love you," Martha said,

reaching down and grasping Bethany's hand before walking

toward the front door. Dante stood still, almost frozen,

helpless even. Both Martha and Bethany looked back at him

with smiles on their faces. "We'll see you soon, Daddy,"

Bethany said as she blew a kiss back towards him. He reached

out in front of himself, caught the imaginary kiss, and as he

always did, placed it gently on his heart. He went to blow a

kiss back to her, but Martha and Bethany had already walked

through the front door.

He turned around and walked to the kitchen counter. He reached down and grabbed the plate and glass of milk before walking into the living room. He sat down on the sofa and placed the plate on the end table. Holding the glass tightly, he looked up and was shocked to see the room was now dimly lit and was actually not his home at all. It was his rundown apartment, complete with peeling paint and sconces lacking light bulbs on the walls.

Dante looked down at his hands; the glass of milk that was once there had been replaced with a near empty glass of whiskey. He knew that what he'd just experienced wasn't real. But, for just an instant, he allowed himself to get caught up in that moment. They were back, and it felt so right. He hadn't felt as empty as he had since they had been killed. He'd felt at home and he liked it. But it was too good to be true. They were gone… he was alone. And that would never change. No matter how much he drank and or how frequently he prayed that it would.

Emotionally exhausted, Dante leaned back in his chair and took the final sip of his drink before reaching out to his side and letting the glass fall from his hand, where it shattered upon making contact with the floor below.

Dante stood up carefully and began to walk to the balcony. Resting his head on the rail, he looked out at the city in front of him. He could see fire bursting from the windows of a building, he could hear screams from the streets below, but he could not bring himself to leap into action. He reached into his pocket and brought out his phone and took note of the multiple missed calls and texts from Scott, Martha's parents, and several others. One from Scott read, "Come on man, you're better than this."

"Yeah, better than this," Dante said aloud, almost breaking into laughter. Standing there in silence, he could almost hear Bethany's voice. His mind traveled back to Steve's funeral when he was asked what they were going to do next. "Change the world, daddy."

Chapter Twenty-Nine

Darkness and solitude had been Seventy-Two's companions for much of his adult life. The two would even manifest themselves into beings who occasionally aided him in his mission along the way, but only when he lost control and was at his most dangerous. He was often seen mumbling to himself, issuing commands to them just before they appeared and enhanced his attacks. It has been a while since Darkness and Solitude had actually been seen, but that is just where he found himself. Alone and in the darkness of the hollowed-out warehouse he'd made his base of operations.

He sat still in the shadows, clutching a leather-bound notebook that showed the effects of constant usage. Crinkled pages and curled corners, the notebook was full of notes transcribed by Seventy-Two. Years of research had yielded plenty of results that he had hoped to find all along. His true identity, his captors, and his family.

Since he'd made his way out of the facility he had been held captive in, Seventy-Two was haunted by gaping holes in the memory of his life before he was captured.

Escaping brought him freedom, but he remained bound by the

chains of his past. He made it his mission to attack the

foundation that allowed the experimentation, abduction, and

ultimately the murder of countless Specials. He also vowed to

fill the gaps of his personal history. He vowed to connect the

dots, reconnect with those he'd left behind, and to make sure

what happened to him did not happen to anyone else... at any

cost.

Seventy-Two's eyes became fixed on a light

that shone in the crack between the warehouse floor and the

rusted metal door. He grabbed ahold of his mask and placed it

over his face, stood up from the chair quickly and turned on

the lanterns sitting atop the tables throughout the room. The

room was shadowed by the flickering light of flames and

Seventy-Two's eyes widened at the sight of his visitor.

"Have a seat. We have some catching up to

do," he said, signaling to the chair opposite him. The man

who'd entered the room pulled the chair out and reluctantly sat in it.

"I've been at this for years," Seventy-Two began, wiping the beading sweat from his forehead. The years had not been kind to him. Behind the mask, his face exhibited newly emerging wrinkles and his hair had become peppered with gray.

"The public and the media have painted a portrait of our kind with me as a villain. How fair is that? I'm the one who was abducted, caged, poked and prodded... yet I'm the bad guy. The very institutions that are here to protect us are the same ones who saw the operation through. But I'm the villain because I struck back." Seventy-Two leaned forward, rested his elbows on his knees and slowly raised his head to make eye contact with his visitor. "Here's the thing about that label. I'll proudly carry that flag. I'll stand in the face of our oppressors and lead the battle for our freedom. If that makes me a villain, then so be it."

"Everything I've done has been out of love for others like us. Every attack, infiltration, and yes... every death was necessary. I'm sure that you are asking yourself... 'Was New York necessary?' New York may have been the most necessary attack of all. Even more valuable than the initial assault in Oregon and the death of Wingard. The attack in New York showed the entire word that we are not to be underestimated or trifled with. Innocent lives were lost... and that would not be the first time... but they all served a purpose. Every step has been meticulously planned and calculated. And, my friend, we are entering the final stage."

He got up from the table the two were seated at, picked up a lantern, carried it across the room and set it atop a large metal filing cabinet in the corner of the room. Setting the lantern atop the filing cabinet. He opened the top drawer.

"This is Oregon," he said as he leafed through thousands of pages of documents. "I was known as Subject Seventy-Two in the beginning. Seventy-Two. That means I was there were at least seventy-one others like me... alive or dead... that were in the same situation I was in. I can only imagine how many more there were after me. And this all happened under the watchful eye of a government meant to keep us safe. Land of the Free my ass," he said as he forcefully slammed the drawer shut.

"Sure, we're different. That doesn't mean that we are necessarily a threat. Our kind have been around since the beginning of time, peacefully coexisting with the human race. Some of our kind began to demonstrate their abilities, and those in power became curious. You know what they say about curiosity, don't you?" Seventy-Two said with a labored laugh.

Grabbing ahold of the lantern again, he also clutched the leather-bound notebook that was laying on top of the filing cabinet. He slowly walked back to the table and sat down.

"Now this...this is what it is truly all about. My memories were seemingly wiped away. I only remembered the facility in Oregon and the things that followed. But I always knew there was more to me than that. Maybe I had a family; maybe I didn't. If I did, did they miss me? Were they safe?" Seventy-Two continued as he began to flip through the pages of the notebook.

He seemed to become increasingly exhausted, the more he spoke. He hadn't slept well in weeks. Every moment awake was spent feverishly planning, researching, and carrying out his attacks. All in the name of his version of freedom and justice.

Seventy-Two's attacks had increased in scale and damage. The number of casualties grew and he did not show signs of slowing down. In the public eye, he was ruthless and dangerous... seemingly never relenting. However, when he returned to the warehouse, he was hanging on by a thread. With each attack and increase in force, he diminished his own powers. Each event required a longer recovery time.

"I had a son, you know," Seventy-Two proclaimed, tears welling up in his eyes. "I had a wife and son.

A family. They took that away from me without hesitation, with no signs of remorse, they just wiped them from my life. I never got to witness my child grow up. I didn't get to teach him to drive... I didn't get to see him graduate," his voice began to trail off.

"And my wife... damn, my wife. We had a life together and they ended that, too!" He said as he threw the lantern against the wall. Debris on the floor began to catch fire and Seventy-Two rushed to it and stamped on it, extinguishing the flames before they spread.

Returning to the table, Seventy-Two slowly sat in his seat and looked at the man who was sitting across from him. "Sorry about that. It's a little hard talking about this. But I have my answers and need to share them with you.

"Where were we?" he asked, flipping through the pages again. "Ahhh, yes. My family. I found out that I was a devoted husband and father. I worked hard to provide them with a life that they could be safe in. I kept my powers and abilities hidden from the public eye, but somehow, they found out anyway. They always find out."

"That brings us to Dante, another one of us. Except he chose to fight for the other side; he didn't have quite the motivation I had. He decided to toe the line and try playing peacemaker. I think we both know that there cannot be peace here. The Civil War that is raging outside is a clear example of that. But Dante continued to play the role of the hero, traveling the world and fighting against Specials like us who wanted only justice and equality-peace for our kind. Dante was a step away from being on our side of the battle, one incident away from being just like me. But instead of joining us, he retreated. His family was taken from him, like mine was from me, yet he cowered and disappeared into obscurity."

The man sitting across from Seventy-Two adjusted his posture and leaned on the table, still covered by the shadows of the room.

"Our most recent battle will not be our final one. I will be the one who dictates that. And that is why you're here. I need you to join me one last time for this final battle. Once Dante is out of the way for good, we can take our rightful place at the top of the food chain. I know where he is. The footage that has been making the rounds has narrowed that down and made his location evident."

Seventy-Two stood up and lifted the lantern to shine on the map on the wall. Red circles and string were connecting locations around the city. One wide circle with a large "D" inscribed by a black marker, indicated Dante's location.

"Once Dante is gone for good, we will continue to advance our cause. I will not rest until there is justice for others like us. I have been networking and building a team of Specials who will join us when the final act of this phase is complete."

Leaning against the window frame, Seventy-Two peered out into the darkness of the city. The black sky was occasionally lit up by blasts in the distance.

"They feared me when even I wasn't sure who I was. I put fear into the hearts of others before I knew just what had been taken from me. They should be even more afraid now that I know exactly who I am. I know what the world has stolen, and I will not rest until I get my vengeance."

Walking back to the table where the man was sitting, Seventy-Two raised his lantern and pulled off his mask. "I was a bit wordy there, wasn't I? I apologize for making that all about me... let's talk about you."

Chapter Thirty

Years ago, a fifteen-year-old Scott Williamson lay on the stiff mattress inside his bedroom in the Children's Homes of Southern California. He had been wearing the same Sacramento Kings t-shirt and tattered blue jeans since his attempted abduction and the murder of his mother three weeks prior.

The other boys in the home didn't say much. They all knew Scott as "the kid whose mom was murdered," and didn't want to get involved with the drama and anxiety that came along with that. Many of the children in this particular group home came from difficult backgrounds. After all, the home was a service for at-risk youth. And Scott certainly fell into that category.

In the early days Scott spent in the home, he kept to himself and remained relatively quiet. Quiet, that is, with the exception of asking for seconds at dinner. His mother always joked with his father that he needed his seconds because "He was growing by the minute." Most of his time was spent mentally reliving the events that led to his being thrust through his bedroom and out into the air in the arms of his best friend.

Scott had a hard time wrapping his head around what he saw. In what seemed like an instant, everything he knew about this world had turned inside-out. He had been a part of a full family unit, had a new "brother," and was genuinely happy. "How could it all have gone so wrong, so quickly?" he mumbled as he lay alone in his room.

"Dante has powers? He can fly? What else can he do?" Scott asked himself. He often wondered how he could have hidden those things from him. They were like brothers, after all, and were constantly together. Scott's internal dialogue bounced back and forth between curiosity and frustration. "And where is he now? Gone... just like that... *where is he now?*"

Miss Margaret, the head of the group home, was the only person who could get through to Scott in the early days of his time there. She saw the anguish that he felt, and she refused to allow the walls Scott tried propping up to block her from doing what she called "God's work." She would spend many evenings before lights-out, reading Bible verses to Scott.

On this particular night, Miss Margaret sat at the foot of Scott's bed and read from the Bible, just as she always did. Normally, he would stay under the blankets with his head on the pillow, but tonight was different. Once Miss Margaret closed her Bible and stood up, Scott sat up and looked at her.

"What is it, baby?" she asked. "You can talk to me."

"Miss Margaret...can you please read Matthew 6:34 again?" Scott asked with a tear in his eye. Scott had become really good at hiding his feelings, using his anger to mask how he felt deep inside. But when she read from the book of Matthew, he felt that he could let his walls down, at least with her. He could let someone else in.

"I sure can, Scott," Miss Margaret replied, grinning from ear to ear as she sat back down on the bed.

The months following this breakthrough were when Scott really began to blossom. He started to cope with the hurt he felt in a constructive way. He joined different groups in the home, from basketball teams to book clubs. He even finally changed that awful Sacramento Kings t-shirt. He was moving on, and that brought joy to Miss Margaret because she imagined that was what his parents would have wanted. She could only imagine the pain that he was feeling, and it made her certain that she was exactly where she needed to be.

As the calendar flipped from 2015 to 2016, a sixteen-year-old Scott was a very productive member of the home and was the leader of several small groups. He relished in the role and truly enjoyed helping others in the same way that Miss Margaret helped him. When Scott turned sixteen, he realized that he only had one year left in the home before he aged out. With that realization, he began looking for jobs and low-rent housing.

He hadn't seen or heard from Dante in over a year... and that bothered him deeply. His emotional wound scabbed over and he was able to mask that pain for the most part. However, from time to time, he would find his mind wandering and he would wonder what Dante was up to. Miss Margaret would tell him to not worry about Dante; she was just sure that he was doing fine. Scott never divulged any information about Dante's powers; he kept that information close to the vest. But he could not help but worry about his friend. He was out there in the world without anyone to look after him. But did he even need anyone else? He could fly, and he probably had a host of other abilities that he had yet to discover.

On a day that was like many of the others that preceded it, Scott was cleaning the dining area when the silence of the first floor was interrupted by a knock at the door. Typically, the door was answered by one of the volunteers, but there was no such response on this occasion. Again, a knock at the door echoed through the first floor and this time prompted Scott to lean his broom against the dining room table and walk through the empty living room to the hallway and then to the front door.

Scott's nerves and anxiety were elevated exponentially. His mind was on alert, and he could not help but travel back to the moment when his parent's home was violated by the men who were clothed in military apparel. He replayed the moment that the door burst open and the flash of light filled the apartment just before chaos ensued.

Nervously, Scott outstretched his hand to the doorknob, but just as he went to turn it, he stopped. He realized he hadn't even checked the peephole to see who was knocking. With an abundance of caution, he uncovered the peephole and gently placed his eye up against the small circular piece of glass and peered outside.

Nothing. There was no one there, and Scott felt embarrassed because of the fear he'd allowed to creep into his head. He had come so far in the time he spent at the group

home, but a couple of knocks at the door had almost undone

all of the progress he'd made. Feeling a swell of confidence,

he allowed his hand to make contact with the doorknob and

turn it as he pulled the door open. The creaking sound of the

door always made Scott feel uneasy, but that feeling of unrest

was gone in this instance. He felt as though he were David and

he'd just toppled Goliath. That creaky door had nothing on

him.

      With the door open, Scott stepped out onto the

front porch and walked toward the front stairs. There were no

packages or notices, much less a military fatigue clad monster

waiting to take him.

      Turning around, he began to make his way back

to the front door just as someone lowered themselves from

the roof covering the front porch. Terrified, Scott fell

backwards and just barely landed short of the stairs. He

blinked his eyes rapidly, still not sure that he saw what he saw.

Dante was hovering just under the eaves, and he lowered

himself slowly in front of Scott, exhibiting much more control than he had the night they flew from the Williamson's apartment.

"HAHAHAHAHA! Bro! You should have seen your face!" Dante said, laughing hysterically.

"Oh, you must be so proud of yourself," Scott said with a tinge of anger in his tone.

Dante smirked and shrugged his shoulders. "Kinda," he replied coyly.

Outstretching his hand to the best friend he hadn't seen in such a long time, Dante's eyes remained locked on Scott's. "Come on, man. You have to admit that it was a little funny."

"I don't and won't. It wasn't funny. Well..." Scott's voice trailed off slightly before he also burst into laughter, grabbing ahold of Dante's outstretched hand. "Where have you been, man? I've been worried sick about you. You could have been here with me. This has been a wonderful place. We could have been getting through this together," Scott said solemnly.

Dante pulled his friend up from the ground and into his arms for a hug, an embrace that both young men had waited such a long time for.

"I had to be away, Scott. I needed answers. What happened to us...to your parents... was a calculated assault, and it could have ended much worse. You and I were extremely lucky..." Dante said before being interrupted.

"Lucky?!? This is what you call lucky? My mom was killed, my dad is most likely dead too. I've been in a group home for the last year, but, yeah, sure, we're lucky," Scott said angrily.

"You and I could have died too, Scott! We are breathing right now. So yeah, I'd say we *are* lucky."

Scott walked back inside and Dante followed behind, closing the door as he entered. "So, where have you been Dante?" Scott asked with his arms folded across his chest.

"I've been looking for answers, man. I've been looking for answers. I discovered my ability to fly the moment that you did. It's not like I was keeping a secret from anyone, I had no idea. And to be completely honest with you, I couldn't be happier that that power had unveiled itself at that moment. We are alive because of it, Scott. Can't you see that?" Dante said, becoming increasingly more defensive.

"So, have you found any answers, Dante? In the twelve months that you've been gone, what have you found?" Scott asked sharply.

"Well for one thing, I have found that I can do more than fly," Dante replied flashing that familiar smile.

Dante walked toward the kitchen and began rummaging through drawers. He stopped at one of the drawers that held the silverware, showing particular interest in the butcher knives. Picking one of the knives up from the drawer, Dante looked at it intently. "What are you doing, man?" Scott asked nervously as he entered the kitchen.

Dante's eyes widened as he lifted the knife into the air. Without hesitation, he spun the knife around, the tip of the blade facing his body now, and thrust it into his stomach.

"Holy shit, Dante!" Scott shouted as he rushed toward his friend.

The smile on Dante's face had yet to fade away as Scott closed in on him. Dante held out his hand and stopped Scott from getting closer. He slowly pulled the knife away from his body and revealed that the blade had bent upon impact, just tearing a small hole in his Los Angeles Kings t-shirt. "There's more than that," Dante said, placing the knife on the countertop.

"More? You can fly and are apparently invincible, but there's more?". Scott asked bewildered.

"I've been helping people," Dante said.

"What do you mean 'helping people'?" Scott asked, his interest now piqued.

"Well, I've been *saving* people actually. Some real hero shit, Scott. I've been out there stopping crooks from sticking up little old ladies on Crenshaw. I've been helping stop gang violence, and I've stopped criminals from robbing banks. It's come with its fair share of risk, though. The first time I intervened in a robbery, I came face to face with a guy who held a gun to my head. At the time, I had no idea that I was bulletproof... or whatever you want to call it. I was scared, Scott. But I knew that I was doing the right thing. Then he pulled the trigger and the bullet stopped when it made contact with my forehead. I bound the robbers together using the chain link fence that surrounded the parking lot, and walked away from that encounter." Dante said while he opened the refrigerator and helped himself to a can of Coca-Cola before propping himself up on the countertop.

"Scott, it was that moment that I knew that I was here to do more than go to college or get a job. I'm here to help others. When the bullet fell from my forehead, I saw a young boy...no older than five years old on the other side of the fence. He was terrified and rightfully so. What if the bullet had taken me down? What would they have done next? They could have gone after him because he witnessed what happened," Dante said.

With a shocked look on his face, Scott walked over to Dante. "That is absolutely the craziest thing that I have ever heard in my life. You've been flying around Los Angeles saving people. You're like a real-life superhero."

Taking a swig from his soda, Dante hopped down from the countertop and stood beside Scott. "Not just Los Angeles, Scott. And we are only getting started," Dante said.

"We?" Scott replied surprised.

"I'm not like you, Dante. I'm no hero."

A lot had changed since those early days. Now, at thirty-two years of age, Scott had seen a lot of things. He'd had his fair share of happy times, many of those were alongside Dante, Martha, and Bethany. But he had also experienced a lot of trauma through the years.

Steve's murder, the battles with Seventy-Two, Martha and Bethany's deaths, Dante's disappearance from society, and now the Civil War which was claiming thousands of lives. Hero or not, Scott had been forced to take up the mantle of justice and peace in the face of hate and destruction. Recent times made it nearly impossible for him to do anything else other than combat the evil in the world, and part of him resented Dante because of this.

"I wasn't made for this, Dante. This was not my calling. The world needs a true hero and I am certain that I am not that hero." Scott said aloud, standing atop a building in downtown Los Angeles.

In the area surrounding him, protesters were clashing with police on the streets, other Specials were battling each other, and looters ravaged local businesses amidst all the chaos. The world was in shambles as Scott contemplated his next moves very carefully. He contemplated swooping down to the crowd of protesters who were violently tangling with the police. He also thought about flying into the sky to take on the other Specials who were battling each

other. This one would prove more difficult because both sides

believed they were fighting for the same cause.

He tried thinking about what Dante would do in

this very same instance. In his mind, he envisioned Dante

appearing from seemingly out of nowhere before interjecting

himself in the fight in the sky. Once he'd deescalated that

situation, Scott pictured Dante flying by the rooftop he sat on,

smiling and waving in his direction as he flew down to street

level. Dante would then stand between the officers and

protesters, and using his words he would diffuse the situation,

because that's just what he would do.

Scott then thought Dante would rush toward

the looters and, using something ridiculous like old telephone

cords, would tie the looters together and kindly restock the

stores and set everything right. After all of this, Scott imagined

Dante flying straight up into the sky and surveying the scene

proudly before he flew off into the distance.

However, Dante was not here. The only clues to his whereabouts were from a grainy cellphone video taken several weeks ago. And by now, Dante had probably caught wind of this video being out and had most likely relocated.

As Scott came back to reality, he surveyed the scene around him and saw that not much changed since he'd begun daydreaming. Explosions could be heard off in the distance and screams soon followed.

As the battle waged on, Scott was taken aback by a figure floating in the air just beyond the fire. He immediately thought Dante had come back to save everyone, but his joy had quickly turned to despair when the figure was revealed to be Seventy-Two. His eyes appeared to be glowing as he maneuvered through the fire and pointed to his wrist.

"Time's up," Seventy-Two said as he vanished from sight.

Chapter Thirty-One

The door to unit 21 was slightly ajar at the end of a dimly lit hallway in an apartment building that looked to be on the verge of being condemned. The numbers identifying the unit were barely hanging with the support of several stripped screws and to give credit where it is due...or not due, some masking tape. Nervously, the man approaching the door checks his cell phone for the time and hoping to see a message saying "Hey, man. I'm good. No need to come check on me." But Scott's phone had displayed no such message. Instead his eyes were met by the light of his phone and the clock display reading 3:12am.

Prior to placing his hand on the door knocker, Scott took another look down the hall down which he just journeyed. The dimly lit corridor was lined with six additional doors which were placed in a staggered pattern from each other. Scott envisioned the person who planned these floors as coming to this decision by placing his (or her) hand on their chin, looking up and down the hall, and saying "Nah, I wouldn't want to see my neighbors' face first thing in the morning, put the doors like this." Surely there were better lighting options than what was used in this hallway, Scott thought. Turning his head back to the mission at hand, Scott raised his right hand and gripped his fingers around the gold-plated door knocker that was affixed to the poorly painted door. As he did this, Scott noticed that the door was slightly ajar and now, an odor became prevalent and invaded his nostrils.

"Man, this is some bullshit." He said as he entered the department. As he walked in, the identity of the stench that met him at the entryway became identifiable now. That smell was unmistakable and belonged to... "Death. Ohhh God, it smells like death in here." Fighting the temptation to empty his stomach of the medium well steak, steamed carrots, and mashed potatoes he had for dinner several hours earlier, he closed the door behind him and flipped on the light switch to the left of the doorframe. Once the light spread across the room, Scott was relieved to see that there was no one lying dead on the floor or the disheveled sofa. But hey, this was just the living room of a three-bedroom apartment, there was still time, he thought.

As Scott surveyed the room, his eyes were drawn to the wall to the left of the television that hung on the wall. This wall was adorned with newspaper clippings and warm photos in nicely maintained frames that were hanging below a light focused solely on that area. It was as if this was the only area that his friend tended to in recent months. Not much dust or dander was to be found in a small radius surrounding the frames hung with such care. Scott walked toward the wall and was overcome with emotion as his eyes scanned over several of the photos.

Just over ten years ago, Scott was one of the thousands of "Specials" who formed a group which focused on protecting communities across the United States from threats "be they domestic, foreign, or not of this planet," as one of the clippings read. Scott was known as Flight. With a name like that, many people surmised that his name indicated the gift he was given was the ability to soar through the skies. Well, on the contrary, one of the powers that he was granted was invisibility. Scott liked to have fun with people and he did so when he chose his code name. The first photo Scott came across was taken at a neighborhood barbecue event with several other Specials who focused their downtime on the areas that were neglected by local officials.

In the photo, Scott was partially transparent and had a young child sitting on his shoulder that was still visible to others while he was smiling and looking to his left toward a broad young man in a spandex suit, which was the trademark of many of the Specials in that day. The man in which Scott was glancing at was pointing toward the camera with a smile that could have lit several city blocks. To the man's left was a woman with timeless beauty who was glaring lovingly at the man in the center while she was holding a little girl no older than 2 years.

Wiping a tear from his eyes, Scott continued to scan over the other photos and newspaper clippings. "Dante

Saves School Bus Full of Children," "Dante Flies to Arizona to

Aid in Extinguishing Wildfire," and lastly "Mother and Young

Child Among One Hundred and Twenty Killed in Explosion."

Scott brought his right hand to his eyes and wiped away the

rest of the tears. "Damn man, I didn't know that all this was in

here. All you had to do was say something. Send a text, make

a call, something," he said to himself as he shook his head.

Scott grew up with the man known as Dante and had seen him

grow into a national treasure prior to his sudden fall from

grace after his wife and daughter were murdered in a what

appeared to be a direct attack which took place at a heavily

publicized event meant to benefit at-risk youth and families

who were struggling to make ends meet.

Scott decided it was time to walk away from the

photos before he spiraled down any further and began to

move toward the sliding doors that gave way to the balcony.

The sliding door was open enough to allow the wind to move

the blinds covering the opening. Standing ever so still, he

glanced around the living area of the apartment one last time.

The table that sat adjacent to a towering bookshelf was littered with pizza boxes, empty and crushed cans of beer, and unopened mail. The television on the wall was off, but there was a faint sound of music that was coming from down the hall, most likely from Dante's room.

Scott slid the door open just in time to see his friend leaning on the railing with one leg draped over the other side. "Dante, what the hell are you doing?!?" He yelled as he reached out to grab his friend before he plummeted 10 stories down. As Scott checked his surroundings, he saw that there were two empty bottles of Captain Morgan beneath the chair that his friend must have been sitting in.

"Scott, could you picture the headlines? Dante Attempts Suicide, but Forgets He is Invincible and Survives 10 Story Fall. What a joke. I'm invincible, but let what was most important to me die. They didn't deserve it, Scott. They didn't deserve to suffer that fate." Dante looked Scott directly in the eyes and with a tear sneaking from his left eye said "It should have been me." Scott blinked twice as if to try erasing the result of the attack from his memory. "You couldn't have changed anything. You weren't even there. Don't you dare put this on yourself!"

Pushing Scott back with a quick shove to the chest, Dante replied "That's the point, man! I wasn't around. I was never around. Yeah sure, for occasional photo ops, but never when it mattered. That's why they're not here anymore. It's my fault." Again, Dante pushed Scott away with just enough force to make Scott back into the sliding door. They both knew that if he wanted to, Dante could exert enough force to send his friend through the sliding door and through the other side of the building.

For a moment, Scott could see a fire in the eyes of his friend that he hadn't been seen a long time. Was it the alcohol or was his friend beginning to realize he was in a battle that is worth fighting? "Bro, I know it hurts. I responded as soon as I heard the blast. Some people hated the Specials so much that they wanted to chop us down by going at everything that made us human. I know it hurts, because I was the one who had to tell you what happened to your family. I know it hurts, because I had to carry out dozens of people who were killed in the blast. And most of all, I know it hurts because I loved them to!"

"But we don't get to run away and hide! We have to keep moving. We have a responsibility. You said it yourself. You've stewed in your own filth long enough. The city is in worse shape than it has ever been in and you're sitting up here drinking it away!" Scott grabbed Dante by the shoulders and looked him directly in the eyes. "It's time to do something about it. Those same people who took your family are poisoning the streets of the city you swore you'd protect and you're just wallowing in your own filth. Man up, Dante. We need you!"

As Scott released his grip, his gaze fell upon the skyline that just lit up as a result of another potential blast. "You can choose to do nothing and let another man feel the same pain you felt or you could grow a pair and bring the fight to the people who fired the first shot." As Scott delivered his message, Dante reached down and grabbed a bottle of Captain Morgan which was not yet empty. Scott knew that Dante had developed a drinking problem after the loss of his family, but he did not realize the extent of the problem. Dante pulled his arm back and launched the bottle deep into the night sky. "Alright man, let's go" he said smiling with a similar grin that was seen at the cookouts and block parties several years before.

Re-energized and filled with a renewed focus, Dante walked from the balcony and into the apartment. He stepped over empty pizza boxes, newspapers, and empty beer cans as he made his way to his bedroom. Dante picked up a cardboard box that was sitting in the corner of the room and placed it on his bed. Opening the box, his eyes began to fill up with tears. Carefully, he picked up the pink teddy bear that was inside and placed it on the bed. He then grabbed the photo album from his and Martha's wedding and clutched it close to his chest before lying it to rest next to the teddy bear.

"Hello old friend," Dante said as he ran his hands over the suit he'd worn into battle many times before. It showed signs of damage, but he smiled as if it were perfect when he saw the red D on the chest plate.

Dante emerged from the bedroom clad in his uniform and the look on Scott's face was one that no one had seen in quite some time. Scott smiled at his friend and hugged him. "Welcome back, Dante. Let's go save the world."

The two went to the balcony and launched themselves into the air, towards the epicenter of the violence. The city had begun to evacuate. Cars were speeding off into the direction opposite to where Dante and Scott were heading. Dante felt comfort in knowing that he was going in the right direction.

Scott pointed to the street and signaled to Dante that he was going to fight at street level. Dante nodded and looked down at the street where Scott was heading. As he raised his head, he was hit with an energy blast that he was all too familiar with. He'd hardly had time to react when Seventy-

Two's fist made contact with his jaw, sending him hurtling backwards.

"Welcome back, boy. I've been waiting for you," Seventy-Two said.

The two flew towards each other and collided violently above the burning streets. Death and destruction surrounded them, but they both felt as though they were the only two in the world. This was how it was meant to be.

With each strike, the ground shook. Dante grabbed ahold of Seventy-Two's head and rapidly punched him several times in the stomach, causing Seventy-Two to hunch over. As his head lowered, Dante lifted his knee and it landed flush on Seventy-Two's face, putting cracks in his mask and shattering his nose, sending blood into the air.

"You're getting weaker with age, old man," Dante mocked confidently. "This ends tonight," he concluded, fists glowing bright shades of red and orange.

Coughing with blood ejecting with each hack, Seventy-Two smirked. "Well, you're right about one thing. This does end tonight."

Dante reeled back and thrust his hands forward and as he did, Scott appeared directly in front of him. Dante's hands stopped glowing and he looked quizzically at his friend. "What are you doing, Scott?"

"What I should have done a long fucking time ago," Scott said as he began to unload a flurry of blows on Dante. Dante found himself unable to protect himself, let alone fight back. As Dante was plummeting to the ground, Scott increased his speed and plowed directly into Dante's stomach and the two both rocketed toward the street.

They landed on the roof of a police cruiser and the vehicle imploded, its wheels flew out on each side of the vehicle. Scott did not relent as he continued to pummel Dante with punches. Scott noticed that Dante was beginning to drift in and out of consciousness.

"No, no, no… you don't get to pass out yet. It's not time," Scott said menacingly.

Seventy-Two lowered himself to the street beside the decimated police cruiser. He held his arm out and Scott backed himself up; and Seventy-Two's arm came to rest over Scott's shoulder.

"What is this?" Dante asked.

"This is exactly what it looks like, Dante. This is family," Scott said.

"What you're seeing now, Dante, is what should have always been. Scott's father wasn't killed while working. He was abducted and used as a guinea pig for sick and twisted experiments. All sponsored by the government that swears it will protect us. I am Scott's father. My wife was murdered that very same night. It took me years to piece together the empty holes in my memory. All the while, I was driven to fight you. It's almost as if, subconsciously, I've always known the truth. I just needed confirmation.

"Oh, remember when I told you that I wouldn't hurt the people you hold closest to you because that was too cliché? I meant it," Seventy-Two said as he slowly removed his mask and looked over toward Scott.

"Don't say it…" Dante began before being struck in the face again. Blood began to stream down his face from a cut above his right eye. This was the first time that Dante noticed that he could bleed, now coming to the realization that he wasn't invincible, after all.

"It was me all along, Dante. The asshole in the bar, Steve, and yes… Martha, Bethany, and the hundreds of others who had to die for me to get to you. I told you that I was no hero," he shrugged. "Now you see how true those words have always been."

Scott handed Seventy-Two a pair of gloves that he quickly slipped onto his hands.

"The battle with Seventy-Two… when I told you that I would protect them. It was all a façade. He was a distraction and I was the instrument of your destruction. I blame you for my mother's death, my father's abduction, and you should blame yourself for your wife and daughter's deaths," Scott said as he stepped away from Dante.

"So, you see, young man... this all started with you. And it will end there as well. I am your end. I will no longer go by the codename Seventy-Two. I am the Omega," He said as the gloves began to glow a shade of blue and his eyes shone a bright orange.

Omega stepped up onto the police cruiser and grabbed Dante by the padding on his shirt, lifting him high above him. "Every attack, every death, and every mission was vital in getting us to this point. This may be your end, but it is only my beginning. I hope you can find solace in knowing you played a key part in all this. Your work here is done, Dante. Rest now," Omega said as he let go of Dante. Dante began to fall back down towards the ground, Omega let off a blue energy blast that made contact with Dante's midsection, sending him flying backward and landing on a pile of rubble.

Laying there, sprawled out on the rubble with his shirt in tatters and his chest and stomach burned, Dante lie there, blood dripping from his mouth, showing no signs of life. Scott and Omega walked over to him to confirm what they hoped to be true. Once they were able to be sure that Dante was indeed deceased, they turned around to see that the fighting around them had ceased as well.

The protesters and police officers stood side by side, the Specials who had been battling in the air hovered in place, many with tears streaming down their face. Dante was gone. Who would save them now?

EPILOGUE

Gasping deeply, Dante woke up, lying on a table in a room completely devoid of light. He sat up gingerly, rubbing his hand across his chest and stomach. Still scarred and sore, he shimmied himself to the edge of the table and let his legs dangle over the side. He stretched out his arms and wiggled his fingers, attempting to make sure that he still had the ability to move his extremities.

Unsure of how long he'd been unconscious, Dante put weight on both legs; he was unable to hold himself upright for long. He collapsed to the floor. The pain was excruciating and shot through his body like surges of electricity. Unable to muster the strength to stand back up, Dante began to crawl straight ahead to where he could see a sliver of light shining on the floor from under a door.

He tried to look under the door, but could not see much, so he pulled himself upright using the doorknob. He turned it and the door opened to the kitchen of the home he shared with Martha and Bethany.

"There he is, Bethany. There's Daddy," Martha cooed while sitting at the kitchen table, eating breakfast with her daughter.

"Daddy! I knew you'd come home!". Bethany shouted with joy.

"You did well, baby. You did well," Martha said as she stood up from her chair and began walking toward Dante.

Taken aback, Dante became overcome by emotion. He knew what this meant. He could now spend the rest of eternity with his family, and there was no place he would rather be. From behind him, Dante could hear footsteps. He peered through the doorway to see who was coming his direction.

A torch was raised high to reveal the outline of a robed person walking in the dark. "Not yet, my boy. Not just yet," The voice said as Dante was sucked back through the doorway and into the darkness. As he was being dragged into the room, he looked up and saw Martha and Bethany standing together in an embrace. "See you soon, Daddy," Bethany said.

"See you soon."

End.